D0710374

LOGIC AND SIN IN THE WRITINGS OF LUDWIG WITTGENSTEIN

LOGIC AND SIN IN THE WRITINGS OF
LUDWIG WITTGENSTEIN

PHILIP R. SHIELDS

THE UNIVERSITY OF CHICAGO PRESS
CHICAGO AND LONDON

Philip R. Shields is assistant professor of philosophy at Carleton College in Northfield, Minnesota.

The University of Chicago Press, Chicago 60637
The University of Chicago Press, Ltd., London
© 1993 by The University of Chicago
All rights reserved. Published 1993
Printed in the United States of America

02 01 00 99 98 97 96 95 94 93   5 4 3 2 1

ISBN (cloth): 0-226-75301-8

Library of Congress Cataloging-in-Publication Data

Shields, Philip R.
    Logic and sin in the writings of Ludwig Wittgenstein /
Philip R. Shields.
        p.   cm.
    Includes bibliographical references and index.
    ISBN 0-226-75301-8
    1. Wittgenstein, Ludwig, 1889–1951. 2. Religion—
Philosophy—History—20th century. 3. Logic, Modern—
20th century. 4. Sin—History of doctrines—20th century.
I. Title
B3376.W564S524   1992
192—dc20   92-16651
                                                      CIP

In memory of my Father

CONTENTS

PREFACE

It was not my original intention to write on religious matters. This project began in an effort to understand Wittgenstein's criticisms of metaphysics, and to show perhaps that there is something philosophically arbitrary in these critiques. I soon focused on two related themes which seem to run throughout Wittgenstein's writings. First, there is a tendency to demand absolute clarity, to demand that philosophical problems should *completely* disappear. And second, there is an enduring and uncompromising commitment to the distinction between "saying" and "showing." This crucial distinction claims that one could not speak or think of what is always already presupposed in any given instance of speaking or thinking, because the sense of what is said or thought in a given instance is always dependent on a prior acceptance of the appropriate logical form. It is this distinction that rules out the possibility of metaphysical reflection and, while explicit in the *Tractatus,* it remains implicit in the later work. These two themes, the demand for complete clarity and the say/show distinction, are mutually supportive, though in different ways. It is the demand for clarity that underlies the need for the sharp say/show distinction, and it is the say/show distinction that in turn ensures the possibility of the absolute clarity of logical and grammatical form. These themes form a kind of system that stands or falls as a whole, and consequently Wittgenstein's critique of metaphysics hinges on whether or not these themes are compelling.

One might easily part with Wittgenstein at this point. One might declare this ultimate clarity a myth or an unwarranted assumption and reject the say/show distinction, thereby liberating metaphysical language from Wittgenstein's critique. However, there seems to be something more to this picture than the individual themes. I began to realize that these themes, which appeared strange and arbitrary by themselves, are part of a familiar picture. Inherent in the say/show distinction are further themes, notions of limitation, dependence, and human finitude. Logical form places a strict limitation on language, and the sense of what is said is utterly dependent on an acceptance of what is shown. These notions are interwoven to form a particular ethical/religious view of the world, a sense that there are powers that bear down upon and sustain us and that we should face these powers with awe, humility, and respect.

At the root of Wittgenstein's critique of metaphysics I found not accidental or capricious philosophical assumptions, but the outline of a religious picture of the world—a picture that is broadly Judeo-Christian, usually Augustinian and frequently Calvinist. The attack on our metaphysical tendencies rests not merely on unacknowledged and hidden assumptions, but on the moral force and adequacy of a particular religious tradition. In this sense Wittgenstein is better seen on the model of a prophet who reminds a people of their obligations than on the model of a disinterested scientist. So I redirected my original project toward an investigation of the nature of this religious picture underlying Wittgenstein's most fundamental and characteristic ideas.

First, I would like to thank David Brent at the University of Chicago Press for his perceptive and untiring assistance. Prior to this there were innumerable people who made my work possible, a lifetime of teachers and friends who touched my life in one way or another, and I could not begin to thank all of them here, but a few acknowledgments are inescapable. I want to express my deepest gratitude to my parents for getting me started, and for teaching me the importance of diligence, of patience, and of having the courage of one's convictions. To my brothers and sisters I am grateful for the years of their love, friendship, and support. For the original dissertation, on which this book is based, I am indebted to many people: to my brother Paul, who first showed me philosophy and had confidence in my work before it could stand on its own; to Richard Bernstein, who first taught me Wittgenstein and continues to teach caution and to point out differences; to Stephen Toulmin, Allan Janik, and Michael Forster for their patient advice and insightful criticisms; to Cyril Barrett and Ben Tilghman for their correspondence and encouragement; to my dissertation advisor, Leszek Kolakowski, for his wisdom, interest, and support; to Brad Brassler and Richard Polt for numerous philosophical discussions and for reading and commenting on various drafts; and to Paul Kelly for his friendship and editorial advice. And most importantly I want to thank my wife, Yan, for her love, companionship, and endurance.

ABBREVIATIONS

CV	*Culture and Value*
LC	*Lectures and Conversations on Aesthetics, Psychology and Religious Belief*
MS	*Unpublished manuscripts*
NB	*Notebooks: 1914–1916*
OC	*On Certainty*
PI	*Philosophical Investigations*
PR	*Philosophical Remarks*
RFM	*Remarks on the Foundations of Mathematics*
RFGB	*Remarks on Frazer's 'Golden Bough'*
TLP	*Tractatus Logico-Philosophicus*
Z	*Zettel*

1

LOGIC AND SIN

AN INTRODUCTION

From calling the *Tractatus* an "ethical" work,[1] to prefacing the *Philosophical Remarks* with the wish, "I would like to say, 'This book is written to the glory of God,'"[2] Wittgenstein consistently framed his technical writings on logic and philosophy in ethical and religious terms. At the same time, these writings themselves do not generally discuss ethical and religious matters directly, and it has been easy for commentators to dismiss such prefacing remarks as isolated and eccentric personal views which have no actual relevance to the philosophical work at hand. The tendency to separate Wittgenstein's ethical and religious views from his work on logic is a natural one and can be justified by the idea that logical validity must compel for internal reasons alone—or more generally, a philosophical work must stand on its own—independent of both external circumstances and the author's feelings.

Wittgenstein had a deep respect for this way of thinking and in his earliest surviving notebook he emphasized repeatedly that "logic must take care of itself."[3] Indeed, this idea was carried to new heights by Wittgenstein and was eventually enshrined in his notion that logical form can only be "shown." However, he also employed this reasoning to justify the cryptic nature of his ethical/religious frame. The ultimate character of his writings must show itself in the writings themselves, and it can no more depend on the personal views of the author, or on any other external considerations, than can the validity of logic depend on such things.

The danger in a long foreword is that the spirit of a book has to be evident in the book itself and cannot be described. For if a book has been written for just a few readers that will be clear just from the fact that only a few people understand it. The book must automatically separate those who understand it from those who do not. Even the foreword is written just for those who understand the book.[4]

In a remark worthy of such a foreword Wittgenstein once declared to his former student and long time friend M. O'C. Drury, "I am not a religious man but I can't help seeing every problem from a religious point of view."[5] While it is not entirely clear what Wittgenstein meant by this, it implies that he thought his work on the problems of logic was somehow conditioned by religious considerations. Those who dismiss the ethical/religious frame as irrelevant are justified, perhaps, but if they do not realize that his writings themselves are already religious even without this frame, then according to Wittgenstein they do not "understand the book."

There has been no shortage of commentators who take Wittgenstein as a religious thinker, who are inspired by him, or who apply some of his ideas to religious matters,[6] but for the most part they tend to be less interested in understanding what Wittgenstein is doing than in using some of his ideas to illuminate, or legitimate, their own religious perspectives and activities. It is perfectly natural, of course, to borrow ideas and concepts from other think-ers, but in Wittgenstein's case this process has obscured or distorted his own actual views. Those studies which selectively use Wittgenstein's remarks about religious belief, or his notions of "grammar" and "forms of life," with-out relating them to his conceptual problems in logic and philosophy, run the risk of making the same mistake made by many of those who, following Russell, tried viewing Wittgenstein's remarks on logic and language without relating them to his ethical and religious concerns. My purpose is to correct both these tendencies by offering a synoptic view of the problems Wittgen-stein addresses, a view which encompasses both his religious and his logical concerns. I am less interested in religion and logic in themselves than in using them to illuminate what Wittgenstein is doing. I do not want to argue that certain aspects and themes in Wittgenstein's work have useful or interesting applications to the philosophy of religion, or to the development of a Wittgensteinian "theology," but that his philosophical writings are funda-mentally religious just as they stand.

Drury frames our project when he asks, "Have I seen that the *Philosophical Remarks* could have been inscribed 'to the glory of God'? Or that the prob-lems discussed in the *Philosophical Investigations* are being seen from a relig-ious point of view?" To argue for the importance of viewing Wittgenstein's work from a religious point of view is not to suggest that logic was not im-portant to him, but rather to suggest *why* it was important. My central pur-pose is to show that from the time of the first surviving notebooks Wittgen-stein treated logical, and later grammatical, form as though it was analogous to the will of God, and in this way logic provided a standard of judgment which was absolute and could serve as a measure of our "sins."

Bertrand Russell was fond of recounting a story about Wittgenstein when he was first a student at Cambridge:

He was not, however, altogether easy to deal with. He used to come to my rooms at midnight and, for hours, he would walk backwards and forwards like a caged tiger. On arrival, he would announce that when he left my rooms he would commit suicide. So in spite of getting sleepy, I did not like to turn him out. On one such evening, after an hour or two of dead silence, I said to him, "Wittgenstein, are you thinking about logic or about your sins?" "Both," he said, and then reverted to silence.[7]

This story is told as a joke, but I would argue that there is more truth to it than Russell ever realized. My purpose is to describe the problems with which Wittgenstein was struggling in terms which show the unity of his preoccupation with "logic and his sins." The idea of bringing together such disparate themes as logic and sin for discussion in a single study may seem both unlikely and perverse. While the apparent incongruity of the juxtaposition cannot be denied, there are far-reaching reasons in Wittgenstein's case for suggesting an intimate connection between them. The unity of his preoccupation with "logic and his sins" not only sheds light on his struggles as a person but points right to the heart of his distinctive way of thinking.

There have been a variety of attempts to understand this preoccupation from an external biographical point of view, ranging from Norman Malcolm's short and tasteful memoir[8] to William Warren Bartley III's controversial speculations about the significance of Wittgenstein's private life.[9] In 1986 the first volume of a restrained and long awaited biography by Brian McGuinness added significantly to our understanding of how Wittgenstein's "consciousness of sin" permeated his early years,[10] and in 1990 a complete and more penetrating biography by Ray Monk, *Ludwig Wittgenstein: The Duty of Genius,* raised our understanding of Wittgenstein to a new level.[11]

Monk's biography offers the most compelling account of the connection between Wittgenstein's distinctive manner of philosophizing and his imposing personality. Monk argues persuasively that Wittgenstein actively cultivated and embraced the role and responsibilities of the "creative genius," taking to heart some of the central ideas expressed by Otto Weininger.[12] Monk specifically mentions two Weiningerian themes that seemed to remain with Wittgenstein throughout his life: one, an "uncompromising view of the worthlessness of everything save the products of genius," and two, a "conviction that sexuality is incompatible with the honesty that genius demands."[13]

Weininger's notion that the life of genius is the only life worth living can be seen as the culmination of an ideology of genius that surrounded a long line of nineteenth-century French and German artists and intellectuals, such as Beethoven, Voltaire, Goethe, Schiller, Byron, Wagner and Nietzsche. In an illuminating study, *Young Nietzsche: Becoming a Genius,*[14] Carl Pletsch shows how the notion of the "creative genius" developed into a cultural phenomenon in which certain "exceptional" and often eccentric individuals broke through the confines and restrictions of academic, religious and social institutions, and defied and mocked the stilted preeminence of aristocratic ideals, on the way to becoming intellectual and cultural heroes, a new elite. In this period, Pletsch suggests, the origin and constitution of this phenomenon remained hidden—the genius was thought to be born, not made—and the stature of these individuals loomed larger than kings in the popular imagination. By showing us how Nietzsche gradually, deliberately and self-consciously donned the mantel of the "creative genius," Pletsch takes a decisive step toward exposing this romantic phenomenon as an "ideology." However, at the turn of the century the genius cult was still flourishing, and Weininger transformed it into a moral imperative—genius or death. According to Monk, Wittgenstein found this imperative compelling, and once Russell assured him that he had talent for philosophy, he deliberately and soberly set about to fulfill the duty of genius.[15]

The genius trope explains many of Wittgenstein's eccentricities. It accounts for his tendency to obscure his own roots, to consider scholarly documentation of sources and precedents unnecessary, to become indignant when expected to abide by standard dress codes and thesis regulations at Cambridge, to reject association with any particular school of thought, and to discourage those who sought to become his followers. According to the nineteenth-century trope, the genius creates purely out of himself, through a process that remains shrouded in mystery. The genius cannot be fathomed or imitated—only appreciated—but the *products* of genius are, like gifts from God, as clear and accessible as sunshine and rain.

While the genius trope operates on a different level from the religious tropes I will describe in this book they can easily be seen as complementary, or at least as compatible. It could even be argued that in Monk's hands, and clearly in Weininger's, the nineteenth-century notion of the genius is itself patterned as a religious, even a quasi-messianic, figure who is concerned with sin and its overcoming.[16] Pletsch is quick to point out the significance of the fact that Nietzsche himself came from a long line of Protestant ministers and originally entered the University as a student of theology.[17] However, the aim of the present study is to investigate the claim that Wittgenstein sees philosophical and logical problems from a religious point of view, and this question can only be settled by an examination of his positions on philosophical and logical issues, not by reference to external biographical and historical evidence. Monk's thesis deepens our understanding of Wittgenstein as a philosopher and a man, and is a rich source of clues for interpreting Wittgenstein's philosophy, but ultimately the philosophical writings must speak for themselves. What still remains to be done, then, is to give an internal account of how logic and sin are integrated within Wittgenstein's philosophy.[18]

Throughout Wittgenstein's philosophical writings there is an expressed concern that all is not well with the world, or more specifically, that all is not well with language. He repeatedly speaks of being "seduced" by logic, "misled" by grammar and "tempted" both by appearances and ideals. One form this deeply rooted apprehension takes is his abiding belief that natural languages hide their true structure, "surface" grammar hides the underlying "depth" grammar.[19] While it is not immediately obvious that such problems deserve to be compared to religious problems more than, for example, to those of engineering or the hard sciences, it is not without justification that Anthony Kenny notes that there is an air of original sin in Wittgenstein's attitude toward language.[20] Whether through an articulation of logical form in the early work or an investigation of logical grammar in his later writings, Wittgenstein endeavors to clarify the elusive inner workings of language "*in despite of* an urge to misunderstand them" (PI, #109). In the same passage he remarks that "Philosophy is a battle against the bewitchment of our intelligence by means of language," and in a similar vein in 1931 he writes that "the very things which are most obvious may become the hardest of all to understand. What has to be overcome is a difficulty having to do with the will, rather than with the intellect" (CV, p. 17).

Such descriptions of the nature of philosophical difficulties suggest that "sin" may indeed be an appropriate figure with which to describe the problems Wittgenstein is addressing, and they permit a comparison to the description William James gives of generic religious form:

There is a certain uniform deliverance in which religions all appear to meet. It consists of two parts: 1. An uneasiness; and 2. Its solution.

1. The uneasiness, reduced to its simplest terms, is a sense that there is *something wrong about us* as we naturally stand.

2. The solution is a sense that *we are saved from the wrongness* by making proper connection with the higher powers.[21]

I will address the second part in Chapter Five, "Writing to the Glory of God," where I describe the character of Wittgenstein's writings as a whole in terms of making the "proper connection with the higher powers," of reconciling what we want to say with logical (or grammatical) form. In the earlier chapters I focus on the first part, "the uneasiness" which says "there is something wrong about us as we naturally stand."

This uneasiness runs deep in Wittgenstein and is reflected in the tone of sobriety in his writings. M. O'C. Drury reports a conversation where Kierkegaard's name came up and Wittgenstein remarked, "Mind you I don't believe what Kierkegaard believed, but of this I am certain, that we are not here in order to have a good time."[22] Wittgenstein's unusual intensity and frequently overbearing seriousness dominates the many personal memoirs of Wittgenstein written by his friends and former students.[23] According to William James this is one of the basic criteria of religiosity: "For common men 'religion,' whatever more special meanings it may have, signifies always a *serious* state of mind. . . . It favors gravity, not pertness: it says 'hush' to all vain chatter and smart wit."[24]

Norman Malcolm reports that it was the artificial conversation of the dining Cambridge dons which so disgusted Wittgenstein and kept him from joining them at the High Table.[25] It could likewise be suggested that it was Russell's relative lack of gravity—or at least what Wittgenstein might perceive as a lack of gravity—which eventually alienated Wittgenstein and which, more than any disagreement about logic, was responsible for the rupture in their friendship and collaboration.[26] I believe this point is important. However, the inadequacy of this suggestion is that it prematurely separates their personality differences from their disagreements about logic.

Wittgenstein's "seriousness" is not merely a personality quirk, a personal and private attitude which could be divorced from the substance of his writings. Granted, what "seriousness" means with reference to Wittgenstein's philosophy is as much in need of clarification as calling it "religious." Provisionally, we can propose that both indicate the centrality of an apocalyptic struggle between the disturbing specter of confusion and degeneracy and a deeply rooted belief in the ultimate clarity and dignity of meaning, as it were, between the forces of darkness and the forces of light. That this is simultaneously a religious struggle and a struggle to understand logic will become apparent.

In this book I propose to give a description of the religious views which appear in Wittgenstein's philosophical writings. To this end I will frequently compare his positions on philosophical issues to themes discussed by various religious writers. However, in comparing Wittgenstein to religious writers I am not arguing for a causal, or even a historical, connection between them.

Some religious writers, like James Gustafson, actually postdate Wittgenstein. As for others, like Max Weber, I have found no clear evidence that Wittgenstein ever read them. While the majority, like St. Augustine, Kierkegaard, Tolstoy and William James, were clearly read by Wittgenstein and in some sense deeply admired by him, there generally appears to be little direct influence. It is usually more the case that Wittgenstein admired these writers because he recognized them as kindred spirits; they each expressed something Wittgenstein had independently come to feel was important. No doubt there are some strands of influence in places, but, with the possible exception of Schopenhauer, Wittgenstein's views of religious matters seem to be fairly well developed long before we have clear evidence of his having read particular writers.

While these comparisons to kindred spirits are not meant to imply a historical influence on Wittgenstein, it is not accidental that most of the writers I will discuss appear to have been read and admired by him. For the most part I want to make a stronger claim than merely suggesting that Wittgenstein *might* be read as a religious writer. Although there are obviously other concerns operating in Wittgenstein's writings, and on occasion there are themes that resist a religious interpretation, in general I believe this reading is the most appropriate one. I want to argue that the religious themes I describe are indeed present and pervasive in Wittgenstein's writings,[27] and that this helps account for much of what is peculiar and distinctive about what he has to say about philosophical issues.

Why, for example, is the distinction between what can be said and what can only be shown put down as the absolute and inviolable cornerstone of Wittgenstein's early philosophy? While Wittgenstein took the say/show distinction as the most important doctrine in the *Tractatus,* its prominent appearance there is often so peculiar and undermotivated that Russell, Wittgenstein's mentor, missed its importance entirely.[28] Part of the reason for this is that Wittgenstein fuses the logical significance of the distinction with an ethical and religious significance that Russell was not looking for.

The following three chapters take us from a consideration of logic to a consideration of sin. In chapter 2, "The Limit," I examine the theme of limitation in Wittgenstein's work and argue that while his means of clarification and his picture of language undergo complex transformations, the uncompromising nature of the limits of language remains constant. The absolute, and specifically Wittgensteinian, distinction between what can be said and what can only be shown is introduced in the *Tractatus* and can be traced through his final writings.

In chapter 3, "The Fearful Judge," I seek to link the theme of limitation to the presence of the figure of God in Wittgenstein's writings. In the *Notebooks 1914-1916,* Wittgenstein emphasizes that "*The limits of my language* mean the limits of my world" (NB, p. 49; also TLP, 5.6), and he describes our position with respect to the world as one of dependence on an "alien will" which "we can call God" (NB, p. 74). I argue that there are distinctive and persistent features of Wittgenstein's thought about language which justify evoking the notion of the will of God. In language he sees arbitrary and inscrutable forces at work which limit and sustain meaning, and which ground our experience of absolute dependence before the judgment of an all-powerful alien Will.

In chapter 4, "The Specter of Sin," I trace the presence in Wittgenstein's writings of the problems of sin, problems ranging from idleness and a corrupt rationality to excessive pride and idolatry.[29] Intertwined with the strong sense of limitation is an equally strong sense of transgression, of our willful violation of the limits of language and our proud refusal to accept our dependence on the powers which bear down upon and sustain us. Throughout his writings Wittgenstein shows how we are guilty of misplaced trust, as it were, of idolatry, when we try to say in words what can only be shown, or when we believe that meaning is grounded unequivocally by pointing either to empirical facts or to mental images and brain processes.

In chapter 5, "Writing to the Glory of God," I discuss the significance of Wittgenstein's efforts to replace our modern compulsion to seek *explanations* with a sense of wonder and awe that is dedicated to producing *descriptions.*

I have suggested that an important consequence of reading Wittgenstein in religious terms is that it sheds light on a number of puzzling features of his writings. First, there are the dramatic and highly touted differences between the early and the later work. I will argue that the popular notion of "two Wittgensteins"—one, the young writer of the *Tractatus* and the adopted father of logical positivism, and the other, the writer of the *Philosophical Investigations* and one of the primary founders of ordinary language philosophy—is based on a serious distortion of both the early and the later work. He did not begin as a logical positivist and did not end as an ordinary language philosopher. If one had to place him in a philosophical school, one would do best to see him from beginning to end as a kind of neo-Kantian. Throughout his writings he employs a distinction between what can be said and what can only be shown in order to eliminate idle metaphysical speculation, or in Kantian terms, he limits knowledge to make room for faith. The continuity of the say/show distinction reflects the continuity of his ethical and religious concerns. While there are important differences in style and method, most appeals to "two Wittgensteins" are premature and end up exaggerating the differences and obscuring important underlying continuities.

Another benefit of this interpretation is that it shows the consistency between the philosophical content of Wittgenstein's later writings and their tone. Why is it, for example, that he who is widely thought to have opened the door to some kind of untenable relativism, to have argued that each word and gesture can be variously construed, goes on to place a great weight or ethical importance on getting their meanings exactly right? The intensity and seriousness of Wittgenstein's investigations seem to be totally out of proportion with the loose "relative" nature of the subject matter. If philosophy occasionally indulges in a little nonsense, what is the great harm in it? Why does Wittgenstein treat the philosopher for original sin? As it turns out, the way of thinking which makes the significance of all human actions and words dependent on the language-games within which they arise, also makes these actions and words rightly or wrongly expressed. They are either in accord or in conflict with the given grammatical forms. The proliferation of language-games does not mean that whatever I say makes sense, but that there is generally a way to judge the sense of whatever I say, to bring to bear an appropriate standard which is clear and final. In this sense, Wittgenstein's way of thinking leads not to relativism but to a form of absolutism which is fully consistent with the tone of moral seriousness in his writings.

My discussion will continually revolve around the question of what it means to recognize that Wittgenstein's writings on logic and grammar are, at the same time, fundamentally "religious." We will seek this recognition in the first place through an examination of the nature, role and implications of limitation in his writings. Themes of limitation permeate Wittgenstein's conceptions of language, incorporating a broad range of traditional religious structures, from the notion that we are dependent on powers which bear down upon and sustain us to the notion that there is an assortment of sins which serve to undermine our proper relation to these fundamental realities.

2

THE LIMIT

Wittgenstein announces the centrality of the notion of "a limit," or "a boundary,"[1] in a frequently quoted passage from the preface to the *Tractatus*.

The whole sense of the book might be summed up in the following words: what can be said at all can be said clearly, and what we cannot talk about we must pass over in silence.

Thus the aim of the book is to draw a limit to thought, or rather—not to thought, but to the expression of thoughts: for in order to be able to draw a limit to thought, we should have to find both sides of the limit thinkable (i.e., we should have to be able to think what cannot be thought).

It will therefore only be in language that the limit can be drawn, and what lies on the other side of the limit will simply be nonsense. (TLP, p. 3)

The idea here is to show what is thinkable by showing what can be said, or more specifically, to set a limit to thought by noting the limit of language. Apart from Wittgenstein's curious qualification of his own words, what is striking about this passage is the prominence and rigor of "the limit." That there is such a limit, and that it can be made "clear," is an assumption which is never questioned in the *Tractatus*.[2]

Even if one accepts the notion of a clear limit, one might still suggest that in Wittgenstein's stipulation "what we cannot talk about we must pass over in silence" the nature of compulsion behind the "must" is ambiguous. On one hand the "must" marks a logical requirement, a rather uninteresting tautology which says that if "we cannot talk" then by definition "we must pass over in silence," since that is what not talking means. On the other hand the "must" marks an ethical requirement which admits a difference in practice between not talking, understood as not making fact claims, and silence, and asserts as an ethical imperative that the one *should* follow from the other. That is, if you are not asserting facts you should not presume to assert anything.

However, as is characteristic of Wittgenstein's thinking, the difference here between logical compulsion and ethical compulsion is not as great as it appears. Strictly speaking, given the Tractarian ontology, neither "must" *says* anything about the world (TLP, 4.462; TLP, 6.41). Rather, they are both "transcendental" (TLP, 6.13; TLP, 6.421). Wittgenstein's reasoning for treating logic and ethics along similar lines begins with the supposition that the world is composed entirely of facts, of accidental and independent situations, and he proceeds to point out that what is "non-accidental," which would include both logical necessity and ethical value, is united in being not of the world. In Wittgenstein's words:

In the world everything is as it is, and everything happens as it does happen: *in* it no value exists—and if it did exist, it would have no value.

If there is any value that does have value, it must lie outside the whole sphere of what happens and is the case. For all that happens and is the case is accidental.

What makes it non-accidental cannot lie *within* the world, since if it did it would itself be accidental.

It must lie outside the world. (TLP, 6.41)

Language can only express what is accidental, facts, so there is no means within the original sentence to distinguish between the logical "must" and the ethical "must." When Wittgenstein asserts that "what we cannot talk about we must pass over in silence," he is not carelessly introducing an ambiguity between two kinds of "must," but drawing a limit which shows the unity of a logical and an ethical demand. This point can be extended to suggest in general that it is not coincidence that the limits Wittgenstein draws have at once a logical and an ethical force.

Here again Wittgenstein's way of looking at things reveals a religious sensitivity. Leszek Kolakowski suggests that "there is a special kind of perception characteristic of the realm of the Sacred. In this realm the moral and the cognitive aspects of the act of perception are so blended that they are indistinguishable from each other: only an analysis 'from outside' produces the distinction."[3] It was our analysis which originally separated the two kinds of "must," and it was by returning to a Tractarian perspective that we made the distinction disappear.

The limit to language, to the expression of thought, which Wittgenstein promises in the Preface, is largely worked out in the text in terms of a sophisticated and frequently enigmatic distinction between what can be "said" (*gesagt*) and what can only be "shown" (*gezeigt*). "Saying" has to do with representing facts, asserting the existence of possible configurations of objects. What is "said" can be compared to the world and must be either true or false depending on what happens to be the case. While the uses of "saying" are fairly consistent within the *Tractatus,* the uses of "showing" take a number of forms which are not easy to reconcile to each other.[4]

In his *Wittgenstein's Saying and Showing Themes,* Donald Harward makes a distinction between kinds of showing which illuminates the difficulties, both real and imagined, that have plagued commentators on this subject. He divides the various uses of showing into two groups which he calls "demonstrative" and "reflexive."[5] "Demonstrative showing" is a "propositional sign," or a "picture," "in its projective relation to the world" (TLP, 3.12). For example, consider TLP 4.022: "A proposition *shows* its sense. A proposition *shows* how things stand *if* it is true." Harward emphasizes that this implies an agent who presents something to an audience. However, such considerations are both foreign to the text and unnecessary. A better criterion would be that demonstrative showing has to do with presenting what Wittgenstein calls "relations proper (external relations)" (TLP, 4.122), what happens to be the case but could be otherwise. "Reflexive showing" is where something simply shows, that is, it shows itself. An example would be TLP 4.1211: "If two propositions contradict one another, then their structure shows it; the same is true if one of them follows from the other. And so on." Here Harward claims that neither an agent nor an audience is required. This may be true, but the determining feature seems to be that reflexive showing has to do with what Wittgenstein calls "internal properties and relations," or "formal properties" (TLP, 4.122), that is, what is essential to a propositional sign for it to express any sense at all.

Harward introduces this distinction between kinds of showing to address a number of textual difficulties. The most obvious is the apparent contradiction between TLP 4.1212, "What *can* be shown, *cannot* be said," and TLP 4.461, "Propositions show what they say." The prohibition against saying what can be shown, Harward suggests, only applies to reflexive showing, whereas the claim that propositions show what they say applies to demonstrative showing.[6] I find this reading unsatisfactory. It not only weakens the prohibition against saying what can be shown, which in turn subverts the clear limit Wittgenstein expressly sought to place on saying, it resorts to this compromise unnecessarily. While the distinction between demonstrative and reflexive showing seems to be a valid and useful one, a more natural resolution of TLP 4.1212 and TLP 4.461 appeals not to the idea that Wittgenstein equivocates between kinds of showing but to the explicit asymmetry between showing and saying.

Although showing and saying depend on each other—neither can occur alone—the nature of their mutual dependence is fundamentally different.

Showing, whether reflexive or demonstrative, has what could be called a logical priority in that both the form and the sense of a proposition are logically prior to its truth or falsity, to what it says (TLP, 4.063–4.064; TLP, 5.551–5.552). Saying, on the other hand, has what could be called a phenomenological priority in that both kinds of showing are properly possible only when in the service of saying. They can manifest themselves only through propositions about what is the case (TLP, 3.3; TLP, 3.314). This is why in order to address confusions and obscurities in language philosophers must resort to "elucidations" (TLP, 4.112), propositions which clarify logical form or sense in the course of saying something about the world (TLP, 3.263).

Now consider how this asymmetry accounts for what Harward takes as an apparent contradiction between TLP 4.1212 and TLP 4.461. The first remark (TLP 4.1212) asserts unequivocally that what can be shown, cannot be said: "Was gezeigt werden *kann, kann* nicht gesagt werden." This obviously is not claiming that a picture cannot be used to say something about how things are in the world, just that what the picture shows, its form and sense, cannot be true or false any more than a ruler can measure itself (TLP, 2.151–2.152). This prohibition is as applicable to the demonstrative showing of the sense of a proposition as it is to the reflexive showing of logical form, and it simply points to the way saying is logically dependent on a pre-established measure which both sets the range of what can be said and specifies a determinate possibility or sense.

The second remark (TLP 4.461) asserts that the proposition shows what it says: "Der Satz zeigt was er sagt." Since showing has to do with picturing a sense, a possible fact, and saying with asserting what is the case, TLP 4.461 should be understood as follows: "The proposition shows [the sense of] what it says [is the case]." This is fully consistent with the claim that what can be shown cannot be said. Pictures and propositional signs can be said because, unlike what is shown, they are also facts (TLP, 2.141; TLP, 3.14). One can only say what is shown in the sense that one can assert that a possibility shown in a picture happens to obtain in the world, and in this sense a proposition must always show what it says, but this is not to allow that the form and sense of a proposition can ever be facts which are in turn represented by propositions.

Our reading finds TLP 4.1212 and TLP 4.461 fully compatible without attributing to Wittgenstein an equivocation between demonstrative and reflexive kinds of showing. When he speaks in TLP 4.1212 of an unqualified prohibition against saying what can be shown, he is referring to both kinds of showing, and the limit this places on saying cuts through the whole of language and aims to determine a boundary between what can and cannot be said which is as sharp and as significant as the difference between day and night.[7]

Those who suggest, following Russell's remarks in his introduction to the *Tractatus* (TLP, pp. xxi–xxii), that the prohibition against saying what is shown can be circumvented through a hierarchy of languages, apparently confuse showing with pictures and propositional signs, which, being themselves facts, are capable of being said by means of further pictures and propositional signs. What is shown can never be said because showing, in Wittgenstein's terms, can never be a fact.

The significance of the notion of showing can be illuminated by briefly considering how Wittgenstein uses it to criticize Russell's 'theory of types.' This is a difficult issue which deserves more attention than is appropriate here. Our purpose is neither to reappraise a thorny problem nor to do Russell justice, but rather to review an important application of Wittgenstein's show/say distinction since it bears directly on the theme of limitation.

In the course of generating the series of natural numbers out of purely logical concepts of identity, class, class membership and class equivalence, Russell discovered a disturbing paradox. Some classes are members of themselves, e.g., the class of classes is still a class; others are not, e.g., the class of lions is not itself a lion. The paradox arises when one considers the second group and asks whether the class of all classes which are not members of themselves is a member of itself or not. If it is, then it is not, and if it is not, then it is. This impossible result suggests there is something wrong with allowing classes of classes without limitation, as was essential to Russell's program. In order to address this paradox Russell introduces his "theory of types," which asserts that individuals and classes are of different logical types which cannot be indiscriminately substituted for one another. Thus "the class of lions is a lion" is not an assertion which is false, but simply nonsense, a meaningless series of signs. In other words, it does not even qualify as an assertion.

According to Wittgenstein, the problem with "the theory of types" is not that what it tries to say is wrong but that it is wrong to try to say it. Whether a series of signs can be combined into a proper assertion, or whether it merely makes a piece of nonsense, is determined in advance by their logical forms and these forms can only be shown. All attempts to say something about a sign's logical form—for example, which kinds of combinations it permits with other signs—degenerate into hopeless antinomies. Anthony Kenny brings out the reasoning here as follows:

The theory of types says that certain types of symbols cannot sensibly be combined: e.g., "The class of men is a man" is a piece of nonsense. But this itself is a piece of nonsense; or rather, it does not achieve what it tries to. For what is meant by the subject of the sentence below?

(A) "The class of men is a man" is a piece of nonsense.

If what is in quotation marks is meant to be just the sounds, or marks on the paper, then the whole sentence states at best a trivial empirical fact about arbitrary linguistic conventions, for there is nothing in that set of sounds which disqualifies it from being given a meaning. . . .

All this, however, is clearly irrelevant to Russell's purpose. What (A) is meant to be about is not the sounds, but their meaning. So shall we say rather the following:

(B) "The class of men is a man," when that expression has the meaning it has in English, is a piece of nonsense.

It seems that *that* won't do, for if the expression is a piece of nonsense then it doesn't *have* any meaning in English. So it seems that we are brought back again to consider the sentence as being about meaningless marks.[8]

Wittgenstein is very sensitive to these kinds of problems, though in the *Tractatus* he generally just gives the results of such considerations. The main conclusions he draws appear in the remarks where he directly addresses the theory of types:

In logical syntax the meaning of a sign should never play a role. It must be possible to establish logical syntax without mentioning the *meaning* of a sign: *only* the description of expressions may be presupposed.
From this observation we turn to Russell's "theory of types." It can be seen that Russell must be wrong, because he had to mention the meaning of signs when establishing the rules for them. (TLP, 3.330–3.331)

Wittgenstein's prohibition against saying what can only be shown is intended to address this problem at its root. Wittgenstein seeks to avoid mentioning the meaning of signs in establishing the rules governing their use by giving an account of language which recognizes that such rules are simply extractions from a sign's logical form and that logical form must always go without saying: "Propositions can represent the whole of reality, but they cannot represent what they must have in common with reality in order to be able to represent it—logical form" (TLP, 4.122). At this point signs must speak for themselves. Wittgenstein writes:

The existence of an internal property of a possible situation is not expressed by means of a proposition: rather, it expresses itself in the proposition representing the situation, by means of an internal property of that proposition.

It would be just as nonsensical to assert that a proposition had a formal property as to deny it. (TLP, 4.124)

This serves to make Russell's theory of types both impossible and unnecessary. With the theory of types Russell tries to express formal properties which can only be expressed by the signs themselves. Thus he transgresses the fundamental limitation placed upon him by language, a transgression we will later argue is imbued by Wittgenstein with both logical and ethical/religious significance.

While first made explicit in the *Tractatus,* Wittgenstein's prohibition against saying what can only be shown is a prominent theme throughout his writings. The religious force of this prohibition is reflected in the fundamental role it continues to play when other aspects of his thinking have shifted or changed their focus. For this reason it will be useful to leave the *Tractatus* and review the appearance of the show/say distinction in *On Certainty,* a collection of the notes he wrote thirty-five years later, long after he modified his earlier way of thinking.

In *On Certainty* Wittgenstein wrestles with Moore's common sense attempts to refute skepticism. He concentrates on two of Moore's writings: "Proof of an External World,"[9] a lecture where Moore boldly combats the skeptic who denies knowledge of an external world by raising one hand and saying, "Here is a hand," and raising the other and saying, "Here is another," and "A Defence of Common Sense,"[10] where Moore makes a list of things he says he knows, for example, "I know that I am a human being," "that the world existed long before my birth," etc. We will call such fundamental empirical assertions "Moore-type propositions."

Wittgenstein finds Moore's responses to the skeptic very provocative. He thinks Moore is right to resist the doubts of the skeptic but wrong to suppose that he can simply assert that he *knows* these things. The fact that we cannot honestly *doubt* Moore-type propositions does not by itself justify a claim to knowledge because absence of doubt does not make something true. Wittgenstein observes: "From its *seeming* to me—or to everyone—to be so, it doesn't follow that it *is* so. What we can ask is whether it can make sense to doubt it" (OC, #2). Moore seems to mistake the concept "know" for concepts like "believe," "doubt," and "surmise," where genuine conviction alone is adequate for correct usage (OC, #21). However, from the truth of the assertion "I believe such and such," one can not infer that "such and such" is true.

Wittgenstein argues that we usually reserve the words "I know" for where the "possibility of satisfying oneself is part of the language-game" (OC, #3), or for when we have "the proper grounds" (OC, #18) for an assertion. For example:

If I don't know whether someone has two hands (say, whether they have been amputated or not) I shall believe his assurance that he has two hands, if he is trustworthy. And if he says he *knows* it, that can only signify to me that he has been able to make sure, and hence that his arms are, e.g., not still concealed by coverings and bandages, etc. etc. My believing the trustworthy man stems from my admitting that it is possible for him to make sure. But someone who says that perhaps there are no physical objects makes no such admission. (OC, #23)

The point Wittgenstein is making is that with a Moore-type proposition there is no recognizable verification procedure, so Moore's talk of knowing is out of place. But for the same reason the doubts of the skeptic can be shown to be out of place as well.

When Wittgenstein asks rhetorically, "Now do I, in the course of my life, make sure I know that here is a hand—my own hand, that is?" (OC, #9),[11] the implication is that *grounds for doubt are lacking.* This is supported by the fact that in such cases the supposition, "Of course, I may be wrong," has no clear meaning (OC, #32; OC, #247). The inconceivability of being wrong is an indication not of knowledge but of the fact that we have neither a reason to doubt nor a means to verify. Real doubting, like knowing, goes together with a complex of appropriate warrants which show how it connects up with other things in our life. Without this the expression of doubts seems not wrong, but crazy: "If someone said to me that he doubted whether he had a body I should take him to be a half-wit. But I shouldn't know what it would mean to try to convince him that he had one. And if I had said something, and that had removed his doubt, I should not know how or why" (OC, #257).[12]

It is not clear what could count as evidence for propositions like "I have two hands," because to begin with, "My having two hands is, in normal circumstances, as certain as anything that I could produce in evidence for it. That is why I am not in a position to take the sight of my hand as evidence for it" (OC, #250). Making the point from another angle Wittgenstein remarks:

If a blind man were to ask me "Have you got two hands?" I should not make sure by looking. If I were to have any doubt of it, then I don't know why I should trust my eyes. For why shouldn't I test my *eyes* by looking to find out whether I see my two hands? *What is to be tested by what?* (OC, #125)

In Moore's case, our certainty that there is an external world is not less than our certainty that "Here is a hand," so the latter cannot serve as a proof (OC, #1; OC, #111; OC, #243; OC, #307).

What Wittgenstein finds most interesting about Moore-type propositions is that we all seem to share Moore's certainty without being able to justify it (OC, #84). Wittgenstein takes this to mean that these propositions play a peculiar logical role in our system of empirical propositions (OC, #136–#138); "I should like to say: Moore does not *know* what he asserts he knows, but it stands fast for him, as also for me; regarding it as absolutely solid is part of our *method* of doubt and enquiry" (OC, #151).

What at first seems to be empirical knowledge, turns out to be indubitable only because it has become essential to the way we live. Wittgenstein observes, "What stands fast does so, not because it is intrinsically obvious or convincing; it is rather held fast by what lies around it" (OC, #144). So many other activities depend on Moore-type propositions that they become hardened into a part of logical grammar. This is why Wittgenstein remarks "I am not more certain of the meaning of my words than I am of certain judgments. Can I doubt that this colour is called 'blue'?" (OC, #126). If we try raising doubts about the truth of Moore-type propositions, this only raises doubts about whether we understand what they mean (OC, #80–#81; OC, #456). Not doubting some things, accepting them as given, is an essential part of learning and playing language-games; "If he calls *that* in doubt—whatever 'doubt' means here—he will never learn this game" (OC, #329).

Once Wittgenstein recognizes the peculiar logical role Moore-type propositions play in our system of empirical judgments, the similarity to formal properties in the *Tractatus* becomes very significant. Wittgenstein's claim in the *Tractatus* that "it would be just as nonsensical to assert that a proposition had a formal property as to deny it" (TLP, 4.124), is reflected in his later claim in *On Certainty* that it is as nonsensical to affirm a Moore-type assertion as it is to deny it: "I know that a sick man is lying here? Nonsense! I am sitting at his bedside, I am looking attentively into his face.—So I don't know, then, that there is a sick man lying here? Neither the question nor the assertion makes sense" (OC, #10). The sick man has become, as it were, an internal property (or feature) of the situation and, in the apt words of the *Tractatus,* "The existence of an internal property of a possible situation is not expressed by means of a proposition: rather, it expresses itself in the proposition representing the situation, by means of an internal property of that proposition" (TLP, 4.124). In terms of the say/show distinction Wittgenstein introduces in the *Tractatus,* these dynamics could be paraphrased as follows: an internal property of a possible situation cannot be *said,* but it can be *shown* by means of an internal property of what can be said. In OC #10, that there is a sick man lying there *shows* itself both in the things being said—like, "He looks a little better this morning," "We must operate immediately," or "Call a priest"—and in the things being done—like checking his temperature, speaking in hushed and sober tones, and changing the bedpan.

Frequently in *On Certainty* Wittgenstein makes explicit references to showing. Consider a few examples:

"I know that this room is on the second floor, that behind the door a short landing leads to the stairs, and so on." One could imagine cases where I should come out with this, but they would be extremely rare. But on the other hand I shew this knowledge day in, day out by my actions and also in what I say. (OC, #431)

That he does know takes some shewing. (OC, #14)

It needs to be *shewn* that no mistake was possible. Giving the assurance "I know" doesn't suffice. (OC, #15)

My life shews that I know or am certain that there is a chair over there, or a door, and so on.—I tell a friend, e.g., "Take that chair over there," "Shut the door," etc. etc. (OC, #7)

That something stands fast and takes on a logical role, that it is an internal property of a situation, is not something one can just *say,* but it does *show* in what one can say. At one point Wittgenstein observes, "Am I not getting closer and closer to saying that in the end logic cannot be described? You must look at the practice of language, then you will see it" (OC, #501). It is strange that he speaks of "getting closer and closer" to the position that "logic cannot be described" when from his earliest writings he emphasized the comparable conviction, first expressed in the opening remark of the *Notebooks: 1914-1916,* that "logic must take care of itself."[13] The continuity between this early idea and his later comment about logic (OC, #501) can best be seen in a remark from the *Notebooks:* "Logic takes care of itself; all we have to do is to look and see how it does it" (NB, p. 11).

Although the distinction between showing and saying is usually associated with the *Tractatus,* we have suggested that it continues to be characteristic of Wittgenstein's way of thinking in his last writings. In *On Certainty* Wittgenstein raises the same charge against Moore's common sense attempt to refute the skeptic that he earlier raised against Russell's theory of types, namely, that *it is a misguided attempt to say what can only be shown.* While it is undeniable that Wittgenstein's later work frequently evokes ordinary language in the course of criticizing what philosophers are inclined to say, the extended example of his treatment of Moore can serve to demonstrate that the operating criterion is not "ordinary language" per se, as is sometimes thought,[14] but respect for the distinction between showing and saying.

Unfortunately Wittgenstein is not entirely clear on this matter and there are remarks throughout his later works where he seems to endorse ordinary language itself as a criterion for determining the limits of language. The most direct example of this occurs in the *Investigations* where Wittgenstein remarks,

> When philosophers use a word—"knowledge," "being," "object," "I," "proposition," "name"—and try to grasp the *essence* of the thing, one must always ask oneself: is the word ever actually used this way in the language-game which is its original home?—
>
> What *we* do is to bring words back from their metaphysical to their everyday use. (PI, #116)

The notion of the "everyday use," or the "ordinary meaning," of a word is both vague and misleading as a criterion for determining the limits of language. Can an application of a word be "everyday" if it is made but once a year? Can the meaning of a word be "ordinary" if it is only used by nuclear physicists? Wittgenstein would answer these questions in the affirmative, and this suggests that the real criterion he is appealing to is not directly linked to how frequent or widespread the use of a word is. Furthermore, he occasionally criticizes ordinary language in a way which shows that it is not "ordinariness" itself which determines appropriate usage.

Fortunately Wittgenstein backs his rhetorical reference to "everyday" and "ordinary" uses of words with a more developed and articulate criterion, namely, whether the use maintains the proper distinction between showing and saying. When he speaks of the "everyday use" or the "ordinary meaning" of signs, the point is that these are generally cases where language-games that determine the form and sense of signs are already in place. Since the grounds for showing have been established, it is possible to say something meaningful. Here language is working and there is little temptation to try saying what can only be shown. This, according to Wittgenstein, is in contrast to "metaphysical" or "philosophical" ways of speaking where the arbitrary designations establishing the form and sense of the signs have not been made—no language-games have been established.[15] Here nothing can be shown, so all efforts to say something meaningful can only lead to confusion.

Our purpose is not to evaluate Wittgenstein's views of philosophy,[16] but merely to point out that in his later writings it is still the show/say distinction, and not so-called "ordinary language," which articulates the limits of language. The failure to appreciate the continuing significance of this distinction has led many commentators to exaggerate the difference between the "early" and the "later" Wittgenstein. The effects of this distortion can be seen in the way such commentators characterize the limits of language.

Many commentators conclude that the boundaries Wittgenstein struggles with change as one moves from the *Tractatus* to the *Investigations*. For example, David Pears claims that they start out as "external" boundaries between what can and cannot be said and end up as "internal" boundaries between various kinds of language-games.[17] While it is true that Wittgenstein becomes more sensitive to the irreducible variety of different forms of speech in the *Investigations* than he was in the *Tractatus,* I would argue that his overriding concern remains focused on the "external" boundaries between what can and cannot be said, and it is as a means to this end that the irreducible variety of language forms becomes important.

In order to flesh out what it means to speak of "internal" and "external" boundaries in Wittgenstein's writings, and to give an idea why some commentators find it a seductive way to distinguish the early and the later work, it will be useful to examine the account given by Pears in *Ludwig Wittgenstein,* where there is a sustained use of this terminology. In the preface to the *Investigations* Wittgenstein says his new thoughts could be seen in the right light only by contrast with and against the background of his old way of thinking. Pears begins by observing, I believe correctly, that the point for Wittgenstein was not so much to compare the new, right way of thinking with the old, wrong way; "His point was that, in spite of the differences between his early work and his later work, what he was trying to do was still the same kind of thing."[18] More specifically, "His task was still to plot the limit of language."[19]

With this sense of continuity suggested as a backdrop, Pears attempts to do justice to Wittgenstein's altered conception of what this task involves. Pears describes the change as follows:

He had ceased to expect the limit to be one continuous line. For factual discourse no longer held pride of place on the drawing board, and, when he did concentrate on it, he found that he was not really able to derive its rich variety of different forms from a single essence. So there would be many points of origin and many subdivisions of logical space. His task, as he now saw it, was to relate these subdivisions to one another by drawing the network of lines between them.[20]

Pears now needs to explain how this can be called "the same kind of thing" Wittgenstein was doing earlier. He continues:

It might seem that this task is totally different from the task which he had set himself in the preface to the *Tractatus,* and that it is only the imagery which creates the illusion that it is a different conception of the same task. For in what way would this filigree of lines resemble the single sweeping line of the *Tractatus?* Surely the line of the *Tractatus* was meant to be the external limit of language, with nothing outside it, whereas the new lines would mark internal subdivisions. What then has happened to the outer limit? Has it any counterpart in the new scheme of things? At least it seems clear that if there is a counterpart, it cannot be the system of internal lines.[21]

With this last sentence, I would argue, Pears' analysis goes awry and rules out the very possibility which best captures the continuity between the early and later work. He gives no reasons for dismissing the possibility that the external limit of sense established in the *Tractatus* could correspond to "the system of internal lines" drawn in the *Investigations,* but it seems he is misled by his own terminology. Pears chooses to describe language-games in Wittgenstein's later work as "subdivisions of logical space." Properly understood, perhaps, this need not contradict Wittgenstein's own way of speaking, but already Pears seems to have fallen under the spell of an inadequate and misleading metaphor.

In spite of Pears' explicit acknowledgement that once Wittgenstein found he could not really derive language's "rich variety of forms from a single essence," he decided that "there would be many points of origin,"[22] Pears' terminology seems to still depict language as a single pie which is "subdivided" into distinct, yet adjacent, language-games. It is on the basis of some such metaphor that he comes to speak of "internal lines" between various forms of language. In speaking of "subdivisions" and "internal lines" Pears is implying that he can grasp language as such, even though he previously observed that the later Wittgenstein considers it an incomprehensible abstraction. It is as though Pears transplanted the notion of different language-games back into the *Tractatus* and the notion of the whole of language as a continuous logical space. This fails to do justice to either the logical autonomy of language-games or the way family resemblances bind them together.

In the *Investigations* each language-game stands on its own, no matter how closely related it may be to other language-games, and the logical space it encompasses is determined from inside through the application of the rules of the game and not through subdividing the whole of language. Thus the limit of the logical space determined by each language-game is an external limit in the same sense as the limit established in the *Tractatus,* which was likewise determined from the inside through the application of propositional form. To speak of internal limits or subdivisions of language is to imply that the boundary of a language-game can be established from *outside* the language-game and that the same boundary can mark the end of one and the beginning of another. However, given the great pains Wittgenstein takes to show the limit of each language-game from inside, it is natural—when seeking to distinguish two language-games he thinks have been confused—that he draws not one boundary between them but a separate boundary for each. Ultimately the very notion of "a system of internal lines" is as foreign to the *Investigations* as it is to the *Tractatus*.

The effects of Pears' misleading terminology can be traced through the rest of the chapter, especially where he contrasts what it means to transgress a boundary in the *Investigations* with what it means in the *Tractatus*. Pears begins, unobjectionably enough, with the observation that in either case transgression means the production of nonsense. Then he muddies the waters by trying to account for the difference between transgressing "internal" as opposed to "external" boundaries.

It is true that there is also a difference between the two cases: For in the first case what produces factual nonsense is simply the crossing of the external boundary, whereas in the second case it is produced when someone crosses an internal boundary without completely crossing it. So in the second case the word 'transgress' has a different and more complex meaning. There would be nothing wrong with really crossing an internal boundary and, for example, using factual discourse about material objects instead of using factual discourse about sensations. The mistake is to try to keep one foot on each side of the boundary, because the two areas of discourse really must be kept distinct from one another.[23]

Pears is right to say that "two areas of discourse must be kept distinct from one another," but he perpetuates the inappropriate metaphor of language as a pie which is then subdivided into contiguous parts when he describes nonsense as "when someone crosses an internal boundary without completely crossing it," or when someone tries "to keep one foot on each side of the boundary." Such ways of speaking do indeed give "transgression" "a different and more complex meaning." In fact, it leads to the absurd position that while a partial transgression is a problem, a complete transgression is okay: "There would be nothing wrong with really crossing an internal boundary and, for example, using factual discourse about material objects instead of using factual discourse about sensations."

The absurdity here can be traced to the fact that it is inconsistent to speak of "completely crossing" or "really crossing" a boundary between two language-games. In such a case one is not *crossing* a boundary—one is just playing a different game. When Wittgenstein remarks that "philosophical problems arise when language goes on holiday" (PI, #38), the obvious implication is that when language goes on holiday it is not going to work someplace else. It is leaving one job without taking up another. However, if language is at work somewhere else, than it is not on holiday, and there is no ground for saying a boundary is being crossed.

In the previous example, the reason there is nothing wrong about using factual discourse about material objects is not that it *really* crosses a boundary, whereas factual discourse about sensations only partially crosses a boundary. The reason is that factual discourse about material objects does not cross any boundary at all, whereas factual discourse about sensations does. This shows the parallel between the boundary of each language-game in the *Investigations* and the boundary of sense in the *Tractatus*. In both the "early" and the "late" Wittgenstein the boundaries he seeks to draw are *external* and their transgression is a matter of serious concern.

This leads back to our earlier suggestion that what makes the irreducible variety of language forms so important in the *Investigations* is the role it plays in establishing clear limits of sense. Those who simply read the later Wittgenstein as a kind of pluralist miss his point. The reason he goes about describing the subtle and far-reaching differences between various language-games is to show that apparent anomalies in language may give way to logics that are in perfect order once one recognizes underlying differences in grammatical forms.

Sometimes what seems fuzzy and imprecise may be *exactly* what is appropriate. In PI #88 Wittgenstein observes, "If I tell someone 'Stand roughly here'—may not this explanation work perfectly? And cannot every other one fail too?" One can only speak of "exactness" within a practice, a language-game, where there is agreement as to the logic of the game, its purpose, and the means for measuring compliance. It is a mistake to suppose that this implies that the rigor of the boundary of sense is abandoned in the later work. The point for Wittgenstein is that although what counts as logical rigor may be relative to a particular practice, given that practice *such a logic is rigorous nonetheless.*

The difference between Wittgenstein and the pluralist is more than one of emphasis. While the pluralist points to the variety of language forms and observes that there is a logic to justify each of these forms, Wittgenstein points to the variety of language forms and observes that there is a logic to limit and judge each of these forms. Once one has mastered the appropriate grammatical forms and recognized which is underlying a given use of language, one can determine what counts as a transgression of the limits of sense.

Before continuing with this theme some consideration should be given to two remarks which are taken by James Edwards as general denials of the claim that language-games are "standards of sense."[24] In PI #130–#131 Wittgenstein writes:

Our clear and simple language-games are not preparatory studies for a future regularization of language—as it were first approximations, ignoring friction and air-resistance. The language-games are rather set up as *objects of comparison* which are meant to throw light on the facts of our language by way not only of similarities, but also of dissimilarities.

For we can avoid ineptness or emptiness in our assertions only by presenting the model as what it is, as an object of comparison—as, so to speak, a measuring-rod; not as a preconceived idea to which reality *must* correspond. (The dogmatism into which we fall so easily in doing philosophy.)

These remarks should be read carefully. The second remark focuses on the dogmatic "*must*" of the *Tractatus*. It does not deny that a language-game can, as a matter of fact, serve as a "standard of sense," but only asserts that such a standard is "a measuring rod," not "a preconceived idea to which reality *must* correspond." While Edwards' sole comment on the second remark (PI, #131), is "Objects of comparison are not standards of sense,"[25] his previous references to "standards of sense" undermine this conclusion by systematically qualifying them with the word "final,"[26] as if to acknowledge the crucial difference between "final standards of sense," which indeed have no place in the *Investigations,* and "standards of sense" which apply to a given place and time.

More significantly, neither PI #130 nor PI #131 is directed toward real language-games, or language-games in general, but specifically toward those "clear and simple language-games" Wittgenstein creates as heuristic devices throughout the text.[27] It is important to distinguish between creating "clear and simple language-games" as objects of comparison and appealing to language-games in which one is an actual participant. Wittgenstein does both, and while the former are obviously not "standards of sense," the latter, it seems to me, are.

Wittgenstein's appeals to actual language-games, while never intended to be the beginnings of a comprehensive natural history, frequently play a very different role in the *Investigations* than the hypothetical language-games he creates. He says he introduces language-games like "the builders" of PI #2 as "objects of comparison" because "it disperses the fog to study the phenomena of language in primitive kinds of application in which one can command a clear view of the aim and functioning of words" (PI, #5). When Wittgenstein appeals to language-games we already practice he expects not merely understanding but, on some level, unqualified assent, which is why he describes philosophy as "assembling reminders" (PI, #127). Later in the *Investigations* he points to the level where such agreement can be found: "'So you are saying that human agreement decides what is true and what is false?'—It is what human beings *say* that is true and false; and they agree in the *language* they use. That is not agreement in opinions but in form of life" (PI, #241). At the point where it can be said that "they agree in the *language* they use," it seems fair to say that "standards of sense" have been established.

When Edwards talks about boundaries in Wittgenstein's later work[28] he seems to confuse the boundary of sense with a boundary that has a sense, that plays a role within a language-game. He bases his discussion on a crucial remark in the *Investigations,* which is worth quoting in full.

To say "This combination of words makes no sense" excludes it from the sphere of language and thereby bounds the domain of language. But when one draws a boundary it may be for various kinds of reason. If I surround an area with a fence or a line or otherwise, the purpose may be to prevent someone from getting in or out; but it may also be part of a game and the players be supposed, say, to jump over the boundary; or it may shew where the property of one man ends and that of another begins; and so on. So if I draw a boundary line that is not yet to say what I am drawing it for. (PI, #499)

Edwards takes this "boundary" to be what has replaced the "objective canon of sense" Wittgenstein articulated in the *Tractatus,* and he goes on to interpret the passage as follows:

In sections 499–500 he is suggesting another picture as more appropriate [than the picture of sense and nonsense given in the *Tractatus*]: judging some utterance to be nonsense is much like saying "I cannot go along with you there." It is to heed or to erect a boundary; and, as he reminds us, boundaries are drawn by *us,* and for quite different reasons. The canons of sense are not given once and for all; they vary at different times, for different persons, and for many reasons. To see judgments of sense and nonsense in this light tends to diminish their apparent "objectivity" and to make philosophical criticism that depends upon such judgments seem much less "scientific," since to make such a judgment is just to call attention to a boundary that someone, perhaps only oneself, has drawn in language for a particular purpose.[29]

Edwards concentrates on one dimension of Wittgenstein's later work which marks a shift from the *Tractatus*—the way standards of sense are formed through human activity and are no longer given once and for all—while he neglects the dimension which marks the continuity with the *Tractatus*—the way these standards of sense continue to stand over and against the will of individuals, constituted through collective practices, customs and institutions that appear as "objective" as natural phenomena to isolated individuals.

In one moment Edwards speaks of how the collective "we" draws boundaries and then the next moment he speaks of how individuals—"I," "someone," and "oneself"—draw boundaries, as if the kind of boundaries collective activities establish is the same as the kind drawn by individuals. Wittgenstein, however, emphasizes that "a person goes by a sign-post only in so far as there exists a regular use of sign-posts, a custom" (PI, #198). Custom determines the games which can be played whereas the isolated activities of individuals, including those who "draw boundaries," generally take place within these games and do not define new games of their own. Wittgenstein expresses this sharply in PI #199.

Is what we call "obeying a rule" something that it would be possible for only *one* man to do, and to do only *once* in his life?—This is of course a note on the grammar of the expression "to obey a rule."

It is not possible that there should have been only one occasion on which someone obeyed a rule. It is not possible that there should have been only one occasion on which a report was made, an order given or understood, and so on.—To obey a rule, to make a report, to give an order, to play a game of chess, are *customs* (uses, institutions).

In his discussion of PI #499, Edwards fails to distinguish carefully between the boundaries of collective practices and the boundaries which can be drawn at the whim of individuals. Thus he concludes from the fact that in the *Investigations* the boundaries of language are determined through human activities that this means these boundaries are no longer "out there" as "objective" "canons of sense" as they were in the *Tractatus*. This, of course, does not follow if one distinguishes between the boundary of a practice and the boundary drawn at the will of an individual.

The "boundary" discussed in PI #499 turns out not to be the *real* boundary, the limit of sense, but only a sign within language. The point is not that a boundary is flexible and can be drawn and redrawn at the whim of individuals, as Edwards implies; the point is that a "boundary" *in itself* (as a sign) can be variously interpreted—it does not determine its own sense. It only takes on a particular sense as it holds a place within a *given* nexus of human activity. This is the point of PI #201:

It can be seen that there is a misunderstanding here from the mere fact that in the course of our argument we give one interpretation after another; as if each contented us at least for a moment, until we thought of yet another standing behind it. What this shews is that there is a way of grasping a rule which is *not* an *interpretation,* but which is exhibited in what we call "obeying the rule" and "going against it" in actual cases.

The real boundary, the boundary of sense, in the *Investigations* is the nexus of human activity, the custom or "form of life" within which the "boundary," as a sign, holds fast.

On this level the line Wittgenstein is drawing between sense and nonsense is every bit as rigorous as the line he drew in the *Tractatus.* It may be more subtle and difficult to discern and it may change over time, but it is a mistake to suppose that the importance and quality of the line between sense and nonsense changed when the one line of the Tractatus was expanded in the *Investigations* to include an indefinite number of lines. To admit the legitimacy of certain seemingly "vague" expressions is not to admit that sense is now on more shaky ground or that the language user is less under the judgment of logical form. To assume the latter is to confuse the spatial indeterminacy Wittgenstein allows in phrases like "stand roughly there" with the unrelenting rigor he demands grammatically: "For the clarity we are aiming at is indeed *complete* clarity" (PI, #133). The difficult question, of course, is what "complete clarity" can mean once one moves from the *Tractatus* to the rambling philosophical landscapes sketched in the *Investigations.*

In *Wittgenstein's City* Robert Ackermann calls the means by which Wittgenstein sought complete clarity throughout his work "one-step hermeneutics." Ackermann describes one-step hermeneutics, and its purpose, as follows:

The meaning of a sentence, if it is a meaningful sentence, can be completely determined by reference to some appropriate fixed horizon of meaning, and the oscillations of hermeneutical theory are then short-circuited. The meaning is given directly because the relevant horizon is immanent in the language that we already speak.[30]

This is also an apt description of the purpose behind the say/show distinction, and it should not be surprising that one-step hermeneutics can be traced from the *Tractatus* to Wittgenstein's later writings just as we earlier traced the say/show distinction. Ackermann writes:

As the map of Wittgenstein's City becomes more complex, the single system of logic gives way to a complicated lot of grammars, but the individual clear sentence, internally related to the world, is always given meaning inside a fixed hermeneutical horizon.

Both logic and grammar must be given completely in advance, or the horizons of one-step hermeneutics would not already exist in order to fix clear meaning. Meaning is determinate because it is created by such structures and not by exploration of the world, Wittgenstein's only transcendental presupposition for the possibility of attaining philosophical clarity. We can foresee what we ourselves construct. In the *Tractatus*, after logic is revealed, the general form of any proposition enables us to work out the meaning of any clear factual assertion. In the *Investigations*, after the grammar of a language-game is revealed, we can resolve puzzlement about sentences involved in the game. Within the boundaries of the clear use of language, boundaries marked by logic or grammar, there is a structure in language that can be known in advance that provides the possibility of completely clear expression. Otherwise, meaning might not be determinate when it is analyzed and might ultimately depend on personal decisions or on private feelings.[31]

Ackermann puts the continuity of Wittgenstein's thought in its sharpest form. One-step hermeneutics illuminates how Wittgenstein could continue to assert after the *Tractatus* that "the clarity that we are aiming at is indeed *complete* clarity" (PI, #133), and how the limits of sense could continue to be sharply defined.

Here we can see more than a passing resemblance between Wittgenstein's "transcendental presupposition for the possibility of attaining philosophical clarity" and the transcendental inquiries of Kant, who should be considered, in Ackermann's terms, the pioneer of one-step hermeneutics. Awareness of this resemblance is not new. In an article written in 1969, Stephen Toulmin emphasizes that from beginning to end Wittgenstein was a "transcendental" philosopher "whose central question could be posed in the Kantian form, 'How is a meaningful language *possible at all*?'"[32] Toulmin observes, "For Immanuel Kant, the central tasks of philosophy were (i) exploring the scope—and the intrinsic limits—of the reason; and (ii) demonstrating the consequences of our irrepressible tendency to run up against, and attempt to overleap, those unavoidable limits."[33] Following the new emphasis given representation by Schopenhauer, Wittgenstein could restate Kant's tasks as "(i) exploring the scope—and the intrinsic limits—of *language;* and (ii) demonstrating the consequences of our irrepressible tendency to run up against, and attempt to overleap, those unavoidable limits."[34] Ultimately we will explicate this irrepressible tendency in terms of "sin," but before examining how the specter of sin is constituted in Wittgenstein's philosophical writings, we will examine the traces of God in these writings.

The religious significance of acknowledging clear human limitations is unmistakable for Kant, as for Wittgenstein. Kant suggests that "our representation of things, as they are given to us, does not conform to these things as they are in themselves, but that these objects, as appearances, conform to our mode of representation."[35] This denial of knowledge of things in themselves serves to limit reason and is clearly intended to eliminate vain metaphysical speculation, our presumption to know things in themselves. When Kant writes that "I have therefore found it necessary to deny knowledge to make room for faith,"[36] he is suggesting that since reason can neither know nor deny God, God is purely a matter of faith. Furthermore, Kant is implying that this result is not merely an incidental consequence of his critique of reason; the emphasis from the beginning is a moral one—"to make room for faith."

One fundamental aim of Wittgenstein's early preoccupation with logic carries through to his later preoccupation with "grammar," namely, to deny metaphysical presumption by recognizing that logical form, and later grammar, determines what can and cannot be said. Seeing the affinity with Kant on this point makes the purpose of the transcendental character of these limits more apparent. It also makes some provisional sense of Wittgenstein's seemingly anachronistic desire to write, "This book is written to the glory of God," in the foreword to the *Philosophical Remarks;* that is, as with Kant, the attempt to put an end to vain metaphysical speculation by charting the limits of reason (language) is a gesture of respect to God (to the value of what cannot be said).

We have sought to show how the distinction between showing and saying articulates a theme of uncompromising limitation which runs through the entire corpus of Wittgenstein's writings. While the enduring quality of this distinction alone is sufficient to mark it as a matter of ultimate concern, it remains to be shown that implicit in Wittgenstein's sense of absolute human limitation lurks the figure of God.

3

THE FEARFUL JUDGE

In "A Biographical Sketch" Georg H. von Wright quotes Wittgenstein as saying that for him the thought of God was, more than anything else, "the thought of the fearful judge."[1] In this Wittgenstein is in the spirit of religious thinkers like Augustine, Calvin, Jonathan Edwards, and Kierkegaard. In Wittgenstein's writings on logic and grammar I will seek traces, not of the kind and gentle father, but of the Law-Giver, and the terrible, demanding, and humanly incomprehensible God of the Judaic prophets—the God who judges individuals, cities and nations and then destroys or preserves them as he chooses, accountable to no one. There are traces of the fearful judge in Wittgenstein's sense of limitation and dependence before the inscrutable ways of logical grammar and in his sense of the contingency and valuelessness of the world.

In a collection of notes by Wittgenstein's students entitled *Lectures and Conversations on Aesthetics, Psychology and Religious Belief,* Wittgenstein speaks hypothetically of belief in a Last Judgment, making a point to deny that this belief is his own.[2] He is interested in belief in a Last Judgment not just as a prediction of an eschatological close of history, which in itself he feels would not be a religious belief, but as a picture which is always before one's mind admonishing one (LC, pp. 53, 56). In such a case, Wittgenstein observes: "What we call believing in a Judgment Day or not believing in a Judgment Day—The expression of belief may play an absolutely minor role" (LC, p. 55).

Here the expression of religious belief can be seen to closely resemble the pseudopropositions about logical form in the *Tractatus,* or Moore-type propositions in *On Certainty.* In both cases, Wittgenstein argues that one cannot make assertions about matters that are constitutive of the means of making these assertions. Pseudopropositions about logical form and Moore-type empirical propositions must take care of themselves. While they go with-

31

out saying, they show themselves in what *can* be said.[3] With regard to religious "beliefs" Wittgenstein makes a similar point:

> Suppose somebody made this guidance for this life: believing in the Last Judgment.
> Whenever he does anything, this is before his mind. In a way, how are we to know
> whether to say he believes this will happen or not?
> Asking him is not enough. . . . But he has what you might call an unshakable belief.
> It will show, not by reasoning or by appeal to ordinary grounds for belief, but rather
> by regulating for in all his life. (LC, pp. 53–54)

According to Wittgenstein, "belief" may come to play a logical or grammatical role which is more fundamental than what can be asserted or denied, and
which only shows by regulating one's life.

What kind of grammatical role might a "belief" in the Last Judgment play?
Wittgenstein mentions that it might be a picture before one's mind which
serves to constantly admonish one. But this only raises the further question:
How might the picture of the Last Judgment serve to admonish? To begin
with, perhaps, it suggests a certain seriousness, that we are not here to have
a good time. Put positively, the picture of a Last Judgment implies that something is required of us, that there are standards by which we are judged, and
that this has something to do with the purpose of life. In spite of Wittgenstein's initial denial, there is much to this picture which is more than hypothetical. In fact, it is just what he says makes the belief religious, the admonishing picture, and not the quasi-historical prediction of the eschatological
event, that he seems, in an important sense, to identify with.

Brian McGuinness observes that Wittgenstein "was glad to have been
brought up to have 'standards'—standards which applied to intellectual
work, to publication, to all cultural and moral matters from the greatest to
the smallest."[4] This shows itself in his struggles for a rigorous expression of
logical form, in his relentless attention to subtle proportions and meticulous
details when overseeing the building of his sister's house,[5] and again in his
highly sensitive and critical ear for music. He was known to be very demanding, both of himself and others.[6] Far from being easygoing and relativistic,
Wittgenstein's own life demonstrates a belief in standards for many areas of
moral and cultural activity that are as unequivocal as the clear standards of
sense we have previously suggested he advocates in his philosophy.

The point here is to see Wittgenstein's strong attachment to exacting
standards, his excessive scrupulosity,[7] as a fundamentally religious sensitivity
which speaks to the presence of God. This is a basic variant on the famous
argument Dostoevsky raises repeatedly in the *Brothers Karamazov:* if there is
no God, everything is permitted. I do not intend to defend this peculiar

reasoning on its own terms[8] but only to suggest that Wittgenstein, who was a great admirer of Dostoevsky, implicitly embraced this reasoning in the variant form: where not everything is permitted, where there are standards and limits, there is something of God.

Although Wittgenstein occasionally raises the notion of God, it never appears as a clearly developed theme. Perhaps this is natural since, at least in the *Tractatus,* he claims such matters are beyond language and should not be raised at all. Whether deliberate or not, this paucity of material makes the task of seeking traces of God appear somewhat speculative. The value of Dostoevsky's maxim is that it links God to the notion of limitation in a way which enables us to address the question of God while drawing on Wittgenstein's central texts. The thought of God as the fearful judge, which von Wright attributes to Wittgenstein, is the thought of absolute dependence on arbitrary power, and this dependence can be seen reflected in the theme of uncompromising limitation.

This approach is supported by a series of remarks in the *Notebooks,* where Wittgenstein explicitly suggests that our sense of dependence points to the figure of God:

The world is *given* me, i.e., my will enters into the world completely from outside as into something that is already there.

(As for what my will is, I don't know yet.)

That is why we have the feeling of being dependent on an alien will.

However this may be, at any rate we *are* in a certain sense dependent, and what we are dependent on we can call God.

In this sense God would simply be fate, or, what is the same thing: The world—which is independent of our will. (NB, p. 74)

These remarks raise many questions, but one point is clear. By linking God to fate and our experience of the independence of the world, Wittgenstein shows that this is not a warm personal God but a fearful Power whose main attribute is His otherness.

Wittgenstein's characterization of God bears an illuminating resemblance to the transcendent Deity represented in the Reformed tradition. In *Theology and Ethics* James Gustafson describes the essence of this tradition as the "sense of the powerful Other, of that on which all things ultimately depend, to which all are ultimately related, which both limits and sustains human activities."[9] This formulation is especially significant because it draws an essential connection between what limits us and what sustains us. As a broad statement of a particular picture of the world and our place in it, this points to an important dimension of Wittgenstein's thinking which cuts deeper than a few isolated references to the figure of God.

In the *Tractatus,* however, there are two senses of "the given," which make it difficult to correlate what Wittgenstein says directly to the description Gustafson gives of the Calvinist sense of dependence on a transcendent Deity. One sense of the given refers to the absolute contingency of each atomic fact, or, taken collectively by the subject, to the total independence of the world. This sense of contingency has affinities with Gustafson's "sense of the powerful Other." The second sense of the given refers to the ultimacy of logical form, the ultimacy of what determines the possibilities of sense. This could be compared to what Gustafson describes as "that on which all things ultimately depend, to which all are ultimately related, which both limits and sustains human activities."

Gustafson's description of the nature of human dependence has a more direct application to Wittgenstein's later writings. One way to mark the shift from the *Tractatus* to the *Investigations* is to note that the two senses of the given we just distinguished seem to merge once Wittgenstein's notions of "the world" and "logical form" are transformed respectively into his notions of a "form of life" and "grammar."[10] These later notions make logic dependent on the existence of particular practices and institutions—they make what happens to be the case the ground for constituting the conditions of possibility, the ground for determining logical form. This is what Pears is getting at when he concludes his discussion of the distinctive nature of necessity in Wittgenstein's later work with the remark that "it is only a contingent fact that there is as much agreement in these ratifications as there is, and it is on this fact alone that logic and mathematics depend."[11] Wittgenstein has a peculiar sense that even logical and mathematical necessities are contingent upon something outside our personal control, upon an inexplicable agreement in judgments (PI, #242). It is this sense which can be compared to Gustafson's description of our dependence on a powerful Other that both limits and sustains human activities. The inexplicable agreement in judgments is like a covenant of God made toward the undeserving. On the deepest levels what is called for is not proof or argument, but a kind of piety or faith.

In his own life Wittgenstein generally saw what he called "the problem of life" as a matter of coming to terms with our dependence on the otherness of the world. McGuinness points out that Wittgenstein saw his periodic thoughts of suicide as evidence of his failure to resolve this problem.[12] McGuinness quotes a powerful passage from a letter Wittgenstein wrote to

Paul Engelmann which describes how, at one of those times when the facts of life were overwhelming him, his thoughts of suicide showed a lack of faith:

In fact I am in a state of mind that is terrible to me. I have been through it several times before: it is the state of *not being able to get over a particular fact*. It is a pitiable state, I know. But there is only one remedy that I can see and, that is of course to come to terms with that fact. But this is just like what happens when a man who can't swim has fallen into the water and flails about with his hands and feet and feels that he *cannot* keep his head above water. That is the position I am in now. I know that to kill oneself is always a dirty thing to do. Surely one cannot will one's own destruction, and anybody who has visualized what is in practice involved in the act of suicide knows that suicide is always a *rushing of one's own defences*. But nothing is worse than to be forced to take oneself by surprise.

Of course it all boils down to the fact that I have no faith.[13]

The graphic metaphor of the man who fears drowning in a sea of doubts is a time-honored religious metaphor which expresses how a man's loss of faith leaves him weak and helpless before the powers which threaten to overwhelm and destroy him.

Wittgenstein uses this metaphor to portray what he considers his detestable weakness—his inability to embrace the world as given and to accept responsibility for what he experiences as the problem of life. Engelmann describes Wittgenstein's dilemma as follows:

If I am unhappy and know that my unhappiness reflects a gross discrepancy between myself and life as it is, I have solved nothing; I shall be on the wrong track and I shall never find a way out of the chaos of my emotions and thoughts so long as I have not achieved the crucial insight that that discrepancy is not the fault of life as it is, but of myself as I am.[14]

Part of the ethical point of the *Tractatus* is that it shows the world is independent of our will. Wittgenstein seems to take this to mean that if there are good and evil, they have to do not with the world but with our will. This assumes that moral attributes are essentially linked to matters over which our will exercises some control. Here the question could be raised: if the world is independent of our will, then why are good and evil not independent of our will as well?[15] While no argument is given, Wittgenstein's choice—to put the world on one side and our will, good and evil on the other side—reflects a commitment to a basic Augustinian theodicy, where evil must have to do with our will since there can be no other source for evil in a world created by an all-powerful, supremely good Deity. However, even for Wittgenstein this does not mean we can, or should, ignore the world. Although the world is independent of our will, we (our lives) are not independent of the world.

Wittgenstein feels this requires us to embrace our life in the world, or in other words, to bring our will in line with who we are.

Wittgenstein sometimes expresses this in the *Notebooks* by the imperative: "Live Happy!" (NB, p. 75; NB, p. 78). In a couple of remarks from the same day that Wittgenstein wrote the passage where he equated our dependence on God, fate and the world, he explains:

In order to live happily I must be in agreement with the world. And that is what "being happy" *means.*

I am then, so to speak, in agreement with that alien will on which I appear dependent.[16] That is to say: "I am doing the will of God." (NB, p. 76)

Wittgenstein is certainly not the first to argue that happiness is linked with doing the will of God, but in his case the argument has a jarring effect on contemporary ears. However anachronistic it sounds, there is something about the notion of "the will of God" which he thinks is crucial and sadly lacking in our modern view of life. By evoking "the will of God" Wittgenstein is suggesting that in an important sense man is not the measure of all things, the world and our forms of life are not of our own making, and there are standards thrust upon us which are not of our own choosing.

In this respect Wittgenstein can again be compared to Gustafson, who writes out of a tradition which emphasizes the awesome sovereignty of God and the severe limitations this places on human choices, actions and aspirations. Consider the comparison when Gustafson writes:

The general direction of moral philosophy is to make man the measure of all things. Indeed, as one moves from utilitarianism in which the consequences of human action are measured—to be sure in terms of their benefits to human beings—to ethics developed from recent action theory, man as the measure becomes even more restricted in scope. Certainly there is nothing like the "will of God" against which to test the propriety of human intentions and actions; certainly there is no longer anything like the moral order of the universe to which human actions are to be conformed. One cannot help but wonder whether this trend of moral philosophy does not itself rest on certain assumptions about the nature of human persons, their liberty and their individual isolation, which might not be factually accurate.[17]

Wittgenstein would share Gustafson's conviction that ethics must be grounded in something like "the will of God," and he does as much as anyone to question "certain assumptions about the nature of human persons, their liberty and their individual isolation." Before examining the role played by the notion of "the will of God" in Wittgenstein's writings, it will be useful to pause and consider in some detail the more perspicuous role it plays in Gustafson's efforts to articulate a "theocentric" interpretation of our circumstances.

In *Theology and Ethics* Gustafson catalogues human achievements in technology, medicine and social organization—achievements such as protection from the cold and rain, easing the damage of floods and droughts through the use of dams and irrigation, developing laws and grievance procedures, eradicating smallpox and reducing the terror of many other childhood diseases, and so forth. Then he points out that this impressive list actually serves to underscore the fact that our lives are ultimately contingent on powerful forces that continually bear down upon us. Each advance brings new unanticipated problems and should remind us that to be human is to be limited. As our powers of foreseeing and controlling the immediate consequences of our interventions expand, our consciousness of our inability to control long-term and large-scale consequences should expand as well. Our knowledge and foreknowledge may increase, but we should see that we are no closer to overcoming fundamental human finitude. Gustafson concludes: "We may not be sure that there is an ultimately sovereign and purposive power governing all things, but we can be sure that we are creatures, and that we are not God."[18]

Gustafson's point is not that it is wrong to try to improve the human condition, but that our efforts generally fail to take the full extent of human limitations into account. We frequently underestimate the hold our past, passions, and physical circumstances have on our lives. We fail to see the extent of human interdependence with other persons, other societies, and varied forces and acts of nature. This blindness gives rise to a steady stream of individual, social, political, and environmental debacles, while fostering the illusion that we can control our individual destinies, or in some cases, the destiny of the world.[19]

Along with the illusion of control, Gustafson argues that we have a highly inflated sense of our own significance in the broader scheme of things. We remain committed to a Ptolemaic cosmology which posits that the entire universe revolves around the needs of the human species and is at our disposal to use and consume as we choose. This implies that billions of stars have been following their courses for billions of years just waiting for the formation of the earth, with millions of plant and animal species evolving and going extinct for another billion years waiting to feed, clothe, and shelter the human species. Expressed in this way, anthropocentrism is comical. For both moral and practical reasons, Gustafson believes it is important to remind ourselves how small and insignificant we are in light of the temporal and spatial magnitude of the cosmos:

> If man is the measure (and not only the measurer) of all things, it is difficult to assess accurately the place of the human species in the long temporal scheme of things, and in the intricate web of the interdependence of things. The anthropocentric focus might even keep us from grasping some significant things about the ultimate power and ordering of life, about the majesty and glory of all that sustains us, about the threats to life over which we have no definite control. The ultimate power is not the guarantor of human benefits; there are many benefits which are ours, but "all things" simply do not work together for the good of individuals and of the human community.[20]

Our Ptolemaic cosmology misrepresents our situation, it disrupts a proper sense of priorities, and it goes hand in hand with the prevalence of what Gustafson calls anthropocentric theology.

In anthropocentric theology the emphasis is on the utility of religion for human well-being. Popular religious movements promise to release us from the burden of guilt, and to give us happiness, success, and self-fulfillment. Few offer to give us new crosses to bear, or to teach us humility before the web of otherness on which we depend. We are told what God can do for us, not what God requires of us. Even for serious theologians like Tillich, argues Gustafson, "the significance of the Christian faith is its reference to a process by which human life, individually, interpersonally, and culturally, is to be 'saved.'"[21] In questioning the legitimacy of anthropocentric tendencies in theology and religious practice, Gustafson is not just offering to reform the excesses of the late twentieth century; he is offering a radical challenge to a dimension of the Christian tradition which has been there from the beginning.

Gustafson does not deny that religious practices may have many sociological and psychological benefits. He just doubts that such considerations are proper and sufficient motivation for religious affections. In Gustafson's words, "The question at issue is not whether religion has some value for persons and cultures; it is whether religions ought to be justified almost exclusively, or exclusively, by their benefits to their adherents."[22]

There are grounds within the Christian tradition for making this critique. The most obvious is that anthropocentric theology seems to compromise the dignity and sovereignty of the Deity. It implies that God exists for the benefit of humanity, rather than that humanity exists as a minuscule part of a larger whole, a cosmos, which is created for the glory of God. Gustafson explains:

> My argument is that such consolations as religion offers come from a deep spiritual consent to the divine governance; that that old defect of hubris or pride is the problem

that correlates with the failure to give that consent; and that much of contemporary instrumental religion is wrong theologically as well as pastorally because it does not set human life within the appropriate limits, not only of finitude, but of ordered relationships in institutions and between persons.[23]

Theocentric theology, unlike its anthropocentric counterpart, does not promise success in human terms. It does not offer a higher standard of living, a longer, healthier life, insurance against natural and man-made catastrophe, and other personal or collective benefits; all it offers is an opportunity to live a disciplined, meaningful life that keeps a respectful place in the larger scheme of things and by so doing hopes to testify to the greater power and glory of God.

I believe Gustafson has described our situation, and what it requires of us, in a way that has close affinities with Wittgenstein's own view of the world. There is a similar sense of the brute otherness, independence, and contingency of the world, of human finitude and limitations in the face of unfathomable power, and of the petty-minded hubris of expecting the world to conform to our will and of presuming that the ultimate power is the guarantor of human benefits. Both warn of the danger of trying to comprehend and articulate the ground of our being, and point to the need for a realistic assessment and acceptance of our limitations—the need for a disciplined, ordered life—as the best way to show respect for what lies beyond these limitations and is immeasurably greater than ourselves.

Our discussion of Gustafson is intended to put the peculiar nature of Wittgenstein's ethics in an appropriate light. Gustafson should prepare us to consider something of the force and radicalness of Wittgenstein's notion of ethics as "doing the will of God." However, comparing Wittgenstein to certain views expressed in Gustafson's *Theology and Ethics* raises a serious question. Do not these views, even the very idea of "the will of God," run directly counter to what is often taken as the most prominent feature of Wittgenstein's later writings, what David Pears calls his "anthropocentrism"? Pears describes this anthropocentrism as follows:

It is Wittgenstein's later doctrine that outside human thought and speech there are no independent, objective points of support, and meaning and necessity are preserved only in the linguistic practices which embody them. They are safe only because the practices gain a certain stability from rules. But even the rules do not provide a fixed point of reference, because they always allow divergent interpretations. What really gives the practices their stability is that we agree in our interpretations of the rules.[24]

Unfortunately, Pears confuses the point by putting the agreement "in our interpretations," whereas Wittgenstein claims that it is only when interpretations stop, when we agree in our "forms of life" (PI, #241) that we have achieved "a certain stability," a fixed point of reference. Regardless, given Pears' more general and defensible point that Wittgenstein grounds meaning and necessity in human practices, it is indeed not easy to see how there is room for any notion of ethics as "the will of God." The natural, and I would argue mistaken, conclusion to draw is that the reference to "the will of God" in the *Notebooks* is from the early Wittgenstein and his so-called "anthropocentrism" marks a later departure from such apparently absolutist ways of thinking.

This conclusion is suspect on two counts. First, we have shown that in spite of sweeping changes in style and a deeper sensitivity to the variety, complexity, and fluidity of language, Wittgenstein's later writings remain committed to the possibility of the complete clarity of logical form, to the demanding rigor of the limits of language, and to the transcendental nature of their transgression. These commitments suggest that Wittgenstein's later "anthropocentrism" does not rule out grand absolutist gestures.[25] Second, even with the "early" Wittgenstein it was never obvious how there was any room for a notion of ethics as "the will of God." In fact, a closer examination of how Wittgenstein spoke of ethics in the earlier period will show that the difficulty in the two cases has a certain symmetry, and that his earlier solution can shed some light on the place of something like "the will of God" in the later writings.

Sometime between September 1929 and December 1930, while still largely under the spell of the *Tractatus*, Wittgenstein chose the subject of ethics for his only known public lecture. Perhaps the most striking feature of what has come to be called the "Lecture on Ethics"[26] is that it does not seem to be about ethics in the normal sense at all. It does not offer a code of conduct or even a discussion of conduct. Rather, as Wittgenstein warns, it takes ethics in a broader sense, including issues like: "what is valuable" and "really important," "what makes life worth living," and "the most essential part of what is generally called aesthetics" (LE, pp. 4–5). To mark this special use Wittgenstein chooses to write "Ethics" with a capital letter.

A cursory reading of the entire lecture reveals that Ethics in Wittgenstein's sense has nothing to do with bringing about one state of affairs in the world as opposed to another. Indeed, one even finds the remark that as a physical and psychological event murder is on "exactly the same level as any other event, for instance the falling of a stone" (LE, p. 6). Before discussing how Wittgenstein reaches these peculiar views about Ethics, it should be noted that Gustafson faces a similar situation, which he expresses by the observation, "Ethics delineated theocentrically [non-anthropocentrically] might not even be recognizable as ethics in the sense that has been largely accepted throughout Western cultural history and certainly in recent moral philosophy."[27] While Gustafson takes this insight as reason to bracket any direct Divine sanction for his subsequent discussion of ethical principles, Wittgenstein goes on to show that Ethics—ethics delineated theocentrically—would defy propositional expression entirely.

In his "Lecture on Ethics" Wittgenstein claims that expressions about what is good, valuable, or really important are used in two very different senses. He calls one "the trivial or relative sense" and the other "the ethical or absolute sense" (LE, p. 5). On the one hand, in the trivial sense we speak of a "good" chair because it serves a predetermined purpose, and apart from this purpose "good" would have no meaning. To speak of the "right" road only means that it is right relative to a certain goal. Wittgenstein argues that these expressions of relative value do not present any serious difficulties for his tractarian vision, because they can be reduced to mere statements of facts where all references to value disappear. Wittgenstein gives the examples: "Instead of saying 'This is the right way to Granchester,' I could equally well have said, 'This is the right way you have to go if you want to get to Granchester in the shortest time'; 'This man is a good runner' simply means that he runs a certain number of miles in a certain number of minutes" (LE, p. 6).

On the other hand, expressions making ethical or absolute claims of value are not made relative to a predetermined purpose or goal. Wittgenstein gives as an example what we would say if he were to tell a preposterous lie and try to shrug it off by saying, "I know I behave badly, but then I don't want to behave any better." We would say something like, "Well, you *ought* to want to behave better." Wittgenstein calls this "an absolute judgment of value" (LE, p. 5), and he is quick to point out that it presents serious semantic difficulties. While he has obvious sympathy for expressions of this kind, they cannot be reduced to statements of facts, so, according to the analysis of propositional form given in the *Tractatus,* they are nonsense.

To highlight the problem with expressions of ethical and absolute value, Wittgenstein gives the following illustrations:

The right road is the road which leads to an arbitrarily predetermined end and it is quite clear to us all that there is no sense in talking about the right road apart from such a predetermined goal. Now let us see what we could possibly mean by the expression, "*the* absolutely right road." I think it would be the road which *everybody* on seeing it would, *with logical necessity,* have to go, or be ashamed for not going. And similarly the *absolute good,* if it is a describable state of affairs, would be one which everybody, independent of his tastes and inclinations, would *necessarily* bring about or feel guilty for not bringing about. And I want to say that such a state of affairs is a chimera. No state of affairs has, in itself, what I would like to call the coercive power of an absolute judge. (LE, p. 7)

In other words, absolute values are incompatible with language because they presume to transcend the arbitrarily predetermined conditions that make language possible. The only expressions of value which make sense are relative expressions of value, and they are not really about value because they can be reformulated as expressions of mere facts. Here again, as with Pears' summary of the central ideas of the *Investigations,* there seems to be no room for speaking of something like "the will of God." Wittgenstein is emphatic that language can only express facts, and mere facts can never have what he calls "the coercive power of an absolute judge"—yet this is precisely what he requires of Ethics.

Before going on to address this dilemma, we can pause to consider the predicament of Ethics in the *Investigations* in light of the distinction made in the "Lecture on Ethics" between relative and absolute expressions of value. Routine value expressions, for example, "This is a *good* chair," or "This is the *right* road," would still pose no difficulties, since they can be treated as expressions of relative value and given analyses similar to the ones Wittgenstein gave in the "Lecture on Ethics." The predetermined purposes, goals and standards which previously permitted the value terms, "good" and "right," in the above expressions to be reformulated in terms of facts, now permit reformulations in terms of following rules in language-games. When someone says, "This is the right way to Granchester," one means that this is the right way to go if you want to go to Granchester according to the rules and goals implicit in our agreed-upon paradigm—for example, according to the way of our forefathers, or the way which gives us the most exercise or passes our preferred eatery; "This man is a good runner" simply means that he performs in a way that compares favorably to the running of those we accept as "good" runners.

Granted, in the earlier case the limits of language were dictated by means of propositional form, while in the current case, as Pears observes, the limits of language are dictated in terms of anthropocentric practices. What is crucial for our purposes, however, is that in both cases there are the conditions for what Robert Ackermann calls a "one-step hermeneutic," where the sense of each expression can be completely determined by reference to some appropriate fixed horizon of meaning.[28] In the *Investigations,* as in the "Lecture on

Ethics," relative judgments of value do not present a semantical problem—they can be given a clear sense—because one can analyze them in terms which show that they are not really judgments of value at all.

Here it should be obvious that the prospect of Ethics faces the same predicament in the later work that it faced earlier in the "Lecture on Ethics." On the one hand, just as a judgment of relative value is not really about value, an anthropocentric ethics would not really be about Ethics, because it could always be reduced to a description of the human activities that fulfill the conditions set by a particular preexisting form of life. Thus, for Wittgenstein, Ethics must still reflect absolute judgments of value, or in other words, it must reflect something like "the will of God." This, of course, brings us back to Dostoevsky's notion that if there is no God, everything is permitted. If nothing has intrinsic or absolute value, then everything is relative to preestablished goals and standards and there is no reference to value at all. So, in order to reflect genuine value, Ethics must have "the coercive power of an absolute judge."

On the other hand, expressions of absolute value are still bound to produce nonsense. Judgments of absolute value are ones that would apply regardless of facts or forms of life. But without reference to appropriate fixed horizons, their senses can never be determined, so "nothing we could ever think or say should be *the* thing" (LE, p. 7). Ethical expressions would face the same basic predicament in the *Investigations* that they did in the "Lecture on Ethics," namely, they would be destined either not to be about Ethics at all or to be nonsense.

Here we have returned to the dilemma we faced before. When Wittgenstein reaches this point in the "Lecture on Ethics," he asks, "Then what have all of us who, like myself, are still tempted to use such expressions as 'absolute good,' 'absolute value,' etc., what have we in mind and what do we try to express?" (LE, p. 7). Wittgenstein suggests a particular experience which, in his own case, seems to typify the kind of experiences that tempt us to try to speak of absolute or ethical values: "I believe the best way of describing it is to say that when I have it *I wonder at the existence of the world.* And I am then inclined to use such phrases as 'how extraordinary that anything should exist' or 'how extraordinary that the world should exist'" (LE, p. 8).

For reasons related to those we have discussed, Wittgenstein thinks the verbal expressions for this experience are nonsense. He argues that it only makes sense to say, "I wonder at something being the case," when it could be otherwise. For example, I can wonder at the size of an unusually large dog because I can conceive it not to be the case, that is, I can imagine a dog of an ordinary size in its place. If I were to say, "I wonder at the existence of the world," this would be nonsense, because I cannot imagine the world not to exist—there is nothing to compare to existence and serve as its measure. Wittgenstein is contrasting an absolute wonder, which cannot properly be expressed, to a relative wonder, which can be expressed clearly.

The example of an absolute wonder[31] does not resolve our dilemma, of course, but it does illuminate our impulse to transgress the limits of sense by showing how the impulse may rise out of a common human experience. While this does not justify the transgression, it helps explain the significance and pathos of the impulse. However futile it is to try to express absolute values in language, there is something about the effort that Wittgenstein finds important and worthy of respect (LE, p. 12; LE, p. 16). Presumably, this respect is not appropriate for many other forms of nonsense—like gibberish, or round squares—a fact which raises the notorious distinction between "important" and "unimportant" nonsense.[30] I am of the persuasion that little can be made of such a distinction, that on this approach the notion of absolute values is too ethereal and elusive to grasp, and that it would be more fruitful to approach the question of Ethics by another, less direct, route which would give us more to work with.

We earlier promised that Wittgenstein's treatment of Ethics in the "Lecture on Ethics" would provide a clue as to the place of "the will of God" in the rest of his philosophical writings. Our subsequent discussion has only shown that, strictly speaking, expressions of absolute value are destined to be nonsensical and that the place for the will of God is outside language. Now I want to suggest that in the "Lecture on Ethics" Wittgenstein juxtaposes relative values to absolute values not only as a matter of contrast, but also as a matter of comparison. There is a crucial analogy being made between relative and absolute values, between the demands of the conditions of sense and the demands of an inexpressible Ethics.

This analogy can be shown by the way Wittgenstein argues along the lines of Dostoevsky's maxim in order to establish the nature and significance of both relative and absolute values. On the level of relative values we can compare the notion, "If there is no God, everything is permitted," to Wittgenstein's argument that if there is not a preestablished standard in terms of which value terms like "right" and "good" can be clearly and completely analyzed, then all possibilities are left open and the words become nonsense. This is merely a specific application of the broader idea from the *Tractatus*, perhaps taken over from Frege, that if sense is not determinate, there is no sense at all. In other words, on this level we are comparing Dostoevsky's maxim to the idea which Ackermann traces through the whole of Wittgenstein's writings, that if there is not a preexisting horizon within which the sense of each expression can be clearly fixed—if there is not the possibility of a one-step hermeneutic—then we can only give one interpretation of an expression after another, and we will never reach agreement. Without "God," understood in the sense of a binding horizon, expressions would mean whatever anyone wanted them to mean, and each interpretation would be neither better nor worse than another.

On the level of absolute values we can compare "God" in the maxim, "If there is no God, everything is permitted," to Wittgenstein's notion of Ethics. In the "Lecture on Ethics" he argues that if value terms like "right" and "good" are not absolute but are made relative to arbitrarily preestablished standards, then they have no intrinsic value or ethical significance, since they are reducible to mere description of facts, where everything is on the same level and has the same value, where murder is neither better nor worse than the falling of a stone.

While there is room for debate over the question whether Wittgenstein would still want to make such an argument later in his life, we have suggested that the distinction between what can be expressed and what has absolute value remains fundamental to his thinking, and that the argument Wittgenstein makes in the "Lecture on Ethics" can be reformulated in terms which span from his earliest to his latest writings. This argument could be put as follows: if the clear sense Wittgenstein seeks in language is dependent on being able to account for all meaningful expressions in terms of preexisting horizons, whether through descriptions of facts or language-games, then "everything is permitted," since such determinations could be transformed into anything with an appropriate shift of the horizons. Without absolute values which hold independent of their horizons—without something like Dostoevsky's God—each world or form of life would be neither better nor worse than another.

This is an odd argument. While structurally it is similar to the earlier argument regarding relative values, which I consider a solid *reductio ad absurdum* argument, it is one level further removed from meaningful experience. Unlike the earlier case, there seems to be no way to test or verify the absurdity of the conclusion, so on this level the premise is unconfirmed, and the argument is inconclusive. *All that Wittgenstein has done is to provide an analogy for approaching the idea of absolute values in terms of the conditions of sense, and it is only on the strength of this analogy that we can speak of the will of God.*

To suggest an analogy between the way Wittgenstein speaks of the conditions of sense and the way he speaks of absolute values is not to say that the preestablished standards, purposes, and goals that fix the sense of relative values are themselves the will of God, but that they are *like* the will of God. In the "Lecture on Ethics," while Wittgenstein excludes the possibility of expressing absolute values, he analyzes the conditions of the possibility of the expression of relative values in such a way that these conditions take on many of the attributes of the will of God. To begin with, the conditions of sense transcend the wills of individuals. They are thrust upon us mysteriously, allowing neither reason, protest, nor negotiation, and they require absolute acceptance if language is to make sense.

A similar point can be made in terms of Pears' description of the anthropocentric nature of meaning in Wittgenstein's later writings. Although meaning in his description is relative to linguistic practices, these practices are ultimately fixed by grammatical rules, or more precisely, by our mysterious agreement in applying these rules. At some point, Wittgenstein argues, "there is a way of grasping a rule which is *not* an *interpretation,* but which is exhibited in what we call 'obeying the rule' and 'going against it' in actual cases" (PI, #201). Though it is the ultimate ground of language, this agreement in applying the rule cannot be forced, earned or explained. Meaning is given like a gift, or a covenant of God made toward the undeserving, and one must either accept it or reject the possibility of meaningful language. Here again the conditions of sense are unnegotiable, transcending the wills of individuals and admitting neither objection nor explanation.

Most of these attributes of the conditions of sense have close affinities to what is often called the *arbitrariness* of the will of God. Gustafson argues that the sovereignty of God understood by the Reformed tradition, as traced through Augustine, Pascal, Calvin, and Jonathan Edwards, "implies the freedom of God to be arbitrary, that is, to not have to render an account of his choices, deeds, and will to anyone."[32] Wittgenstein recognizes explicitly, in a remark from the *Investigations,* that it is just such arbitrariness which grounds the analogy between absolute values and grammatical rules:

Consider: "The only correlate in language to an intrinsic necessity is an arbitrary rule. It is the only thing which one can milk out of this intrinsic necessity into a proposition." (PI, #372)[32]

In a way that bears comparison to the arbitrariness of the will of God, that which limits and sustains meaning is arbitrary and does "not have to render an account of [its] choices, deeds, and will to anyone."

We should no more expect an explanation or justification of logical grammar than Jonathan Edwards would expect an explanation of God's guidance of earthly affairs. In either case the proper thing to do is to give a *description*. In another passage from the *Investigations* Wittgenstein puts it like this:

Grammar does not tell us how language must be constructed in order to fulfil its purpose, in order to have such-and-such an effect on human beings. It only describes and in no way explains the use of signs.

The rules of grammar may be called "arbitrary" [*Willkürlich*], if that is to mean that the *aim* of the grammar is nothing but that of the language. (PI, #496–#497)

I take this last remark to be saying that the rules of grammar are not arbitrary in the sense of being either aimless or capricious. First, there is a sense of being arbitrary which means "random," but it is obvious that grammar has direction, albeit an internal one, so this must not be the sense Wittgenstein has in mind. Second, a common use of "arbitrary" does in fact imply a certain negligence or malice, as when we normally apply it to anyone in authority, like a parent, a teacher, or a government official. In these cases it usually means that the persons are acting according to their own will without regard for the higher principles, or formal procedures, which are considered appropriate standards for their stations. Wittgenstein is only acknowledging that grammar is arbitrary in the sense that it follows its own purposes without regard for any higher purpose, but he denies that this involves a shortcoming or reproach since grammar, unlike parents, teachers and officials, has no higher purpose external to itself. Grammar is, in a manner of speaking, the measure of all things, so there is no way to contrast grammar's purposes with what it *should* be aiming toward.

We have suggested that an appropriate analogy for the arbitrariness of grammar is the arbitrariness of the will of God. We are now in a position to show how distinctive the comparison is by taking a closer look at what it means to speak of the arbitrariness of the will of God. Martin Luther writes:

God is He for Whose will no cause or ground may be laid down as its rule and standard; for nothing is on a level with it or above it, but it is itself the rule for all things. If any rule or standard, or cause or ground, existed for it, it could no longer be the will of God. What God wills is not right because He ought, or was bound, so to will; on the contrary, what takes place must be right, because He so wills it. Causes and grounds are laid down for the will of the creature, but not for the will of the Creator—unless you set another Creator over Him![33]

This account describes the specific sense of being arbitrary we developed to describe Wittgenstein's notion of grammar. God's purposes are given without reason or justification, yet they cannot properly be considered capricious because there is no higher external standard by which to judge the will of God.

Luther's statement is a powerful expression of one side of a debate going back at least to Socrates: Are God's commands right because he commands them, or does he command them because they are right? There are those like Aquinas and Leibniz who follow Socrates and argue against the arbitrariness of the will of God. And there are others, like Augustine, Pascal, and Kierkegaard, who are deeply suspicious of reason and hold with Luther that God's commands are right simply because he so commands. Gustafson argues that the Socratic choice ultimately makes God subservient to the dictates of human reason and leads us to an anthropocentric ethics which has lost any serious notion of doing the will of God.[34]

A test case, which pits reason against the will of God, is the story of Abraham's willingness to follow God's command to sacrifice his only son Isaac.[35] This command, discussed in depth by Kierkegaard in *Fear and Trembling*,[36] defies all anthropocentric ethical principles and has no apparent relation to human well being. Furthermore, it flies directly in the face of God's prior promise to make of Abraham a great nation, which means that it not only defies human morality, but it also defies Reason. Kierkegaard argues that it is just such absurdity which marks the will of God and presents a genuine opportunity for faith. For Kierkegaard, one cannot act reasonably and religiously at the same time, since as soon as one acts for reasons one is not acting simply because it is the will of God. This way of putting the matter closely resembles Wittgenstein's claim in the "Lecture on Ethics" that values which are relative to preexisting standards are not really values, that an instrumental or relative ethics is not really Ethics.

When the debate over whether or not God is bound by reason is raised in terms of ethics by Moritz Schlick, Wittgenstein naturally sides with those who hold that ethics is grounded in the will of God, not in reason. In this way Wittgenstein hopes to acknowledge from the start our ultimate dependence on arbitrary powers. Friedrich Waismann quotes Wittgenstein's response:

Schlick says that theological ethics contains two conceptions of the essence of the Good. According to the more superficial interpretation, the Good is good because God wills it; according to the deeper interpretation, God wills the Good because it is good.

I think that the first conception is the deeper one: Good is what God orders. For this cuts off the path to any and every explanation 'why' it is good, while the second conception is precisely the superficial, the rationalistic one, which proceeds as if what is good could still be given some foundation.

The first conception says clearly that the essence of the Good has nothing to do with facts and therefore cannot be explained by any proposition. If any proposition expresses just what I mean, it is: Good is what God orders."[37]

It is obvious that making the Good dependent on the will of God does not make it arbitrary in the sense of being random and without direction, but rather it is only to say that the Good is arrived at without allowing argument or objection.

The crucial point I am trying to make here is reflected in the fact that "arbitrary" and "arbitrate" have a common root. The derivation of the English word "arbitrary" is from the Latin *arbitrarius,* which is closely related to the Latin *arbiter,* meaning "judge," or "umpire." A judge decided ambiguities and ends disputes.[38] Wittgenstein is continually trying to show how logical grammar is arbitrary in this precise sense.

When Wittgenstein suggests that "Good is what God orders," it can be seen as a specific case, perhaps a paradigmatic case, of rule following in general. For example, with regard to following a mathematical formula, he observes, "When someone whom I am afraid of orders me to continue the series, I act quickly, with perfect certainty, and the lack of reasons does not trouble me" (PI, #212). The point here could be put more bluntly as follows: "When I obey a rule, I do not choose. I obey the rule *blindly*" (PI, #218). If this produces a sense of vertigo, it is probably being misconstrued. Following a rule blindly does not imply that the rule is followed randomly, or with groping hesitation and indecisiveness. On the contrary, it means that the rule is followed with a kind of immediacy, without considering other possible applications or interpretations. The same idea is expressed in another controversial remark: "If I have exhausted the justifications I have reached bedrock and my spade is turned. Then I am inclined to say: 'This is simply what I do'" (PI, #217). Here further objections and demands for explanation are superfluous, not because "anything goes" but because the matter is settled. The crucial point, for Wittgenstein, is that "there is a way of grasping a rule which is *not* an *interpretation,* but which is exhibited in what we call 'obeying the rule' and 'going against it' in actual cases" (PI, #201).

Framing the remark quoted earlier from *Investigations* #372, where Wittgenstein compares intrinsic necessity to an arbitrary rule, there are two remarks about grammar. The first says, "Essence is expressed by grammar"

(PI, #371), and the second says, "Grammar tells what kind of object anything is. (Theology as grammar)" (PI, #373). These remarks point to the
fundamental role grammar plays in constituting our language and our world.
Although grammar consists of arbitrary rules, human beings agree on these
rules, and "that is not agreement in opinions but in forms of life" (PI, #241).
This is the basis for Wittgenstein's enigmatic remark: "If one tried to advance
theses in philosophy, it would never be possible to debate them, because everyone would agree to them" (PI, #128). Philosophical theses would presumably have to do with things like essences and ontology, and it is just these
kinds of matters that are established beforehand by grammar, by sharing a
common language. Wittgenstein seems to suggest that the claim, "Grammar
tells what kind of object anything is," is analogous to saying that "Good is
what God orders." Both involve a determination that is "arrived at without
allowing argument or objection." The dictates of logical grammar are thrust
upon us as if they were the will of God.

When Wittgenstein makes the cryptic parenthetical remark "(Theology
as grammar)," he implies that theology could be construed as an attempt to
describe the grammatical rules for talking about God.[39] Our discussion above
suggests that one can also turn it around and take grammar as theology, as
the study of the will of God. Such a study would seem to have the same use
and limitations as a study of the story of Abraham's near sacrifice of Isaac.
The use is that the study would show our absolute dependence on the arbitrary powers that bear down upon and sustain us. The limitation is that, even
if grammar were taken as the will of God, one could no more extract any
general laws regarding the goodness of rules of grammar than one can extract
any general principles regarding the goodness of sacrificing one's children
from the story of Abraham and Isaac.

The presence of an analogy between the standards of sense and the will of
God is the basis of our general thesis that Wittgenstein's writings are religious
just as they stand. I have described this analogy in terms that largely derive
from particular religious traditions which are suspicious of human reason and
place great emphasis on the sovereignty and inscrutability of the will of God.
Without meaning to neglect or diminish the obvious religious, philosophical,
and historical significance of other religious traditions, like those which hold
to a belief in a God of Reason, I have set them aside. When I speak of reading
Wittgenstein as a religious thinker, I am understanding him in terms of those
particular religious traditions which emphasize our finitude and utter dependence on the will of God, traditions exemplified by the likes of Augustine,

Pascal, Luther, and Kierkegaard. Although our discussion has drawn heavily on Christian writers, it is significant that the notion of the absolute sovereignty of God has its roots in ancient Judaism. It seems Wittgenstein was attracted to the dimension of Christianity which most resembled the faith of his ancestors.

In chapter 2, I suggested that the whole of Wittgenstein's writings could be characterized by an effort to articulate the limits of language in terms of a sharp distinction between saying and showing. In the present chapter, I have sought to develop the idea that these limits are meant to have a clarity and rigor that are as uncompromising as the will of God. I have suggested that Wittgenstein's notion of God as "the fearful judge" represents the "arbitrariness" of grammar. It represents the fact that there is a way of following a rule which is not an interpretation, a way of uncontrolled power and authority that is "arrived at without allowing argument or objection." In the face of the prospect of perpetual interpretation, Wittgenstein's interest in the Last Judgment can be understood in terms of his commitment to the omnipresence of a one-step hermeneutic, where a clear terminus can always be produced in terms of a given horizon—where the questions, arguments, and interpretations come to an end and he can say, "I have reached bedrock, and my spade is turned." But by the same analogy, the conditions for the possibility of the determinacy of sense imply something about the nature of Deity. The arbitrariness of grammar shows us what it means to speak of the arbitrariness of the will of God.

4

THE SPECTER OF SIN

In this chapter I will try to show that the standard reading which views Wittgenstein's treatment of philosophical problems in terms of "illusions"— a metaphor Wittgenstein mentions himself—is generally inadequate, and that his occasional references to sin suggest a more penetrating and comprehensive means of understanding the peculiarities and intricacies of his work. To begin with, I will concentrate most directly on Wittgenstein's later writings, where these themes seem to find their fullest expression, but at key points I will trace their continuity with his earlier thought.

The *Philosophical Investigations* abound with rich and incisive discussions of various kinds of philosophical transgressions and temptations. There are obvious affinities to Kant's attributing the interminableness of "metaphysical" disputes to various ways in which human reason overreaches its appropriate bounds, but Wittgenstein never attempts to generate a systematic and comprehensive classification, along the lines of Kant's transcendental dialectic, of the sources of these errors. Given the unsystematic nature of Wittgenstein's later work, it is hard to survey the many kinds of philosophical problems he discusses there. In *Insight and Illusion,* P. M. S. Hacker offers us a representative list, which denies any pretensions to completeness, of the main sources of metaphysical illusions Wittgenstein describes in his later works.[1] Since Hacker's reading is well developed, and fairly characteristic of what I would consider the received interpretation, I will consider his reading in some detail. Ultimately, I do not intend to dispute the specifics of this reading but only to place the standard themes within a particular religious frame which gives them a deeper significance.

The five sources of philosophical problems mentioned by Hacker are as follows: "(1) superficial analogies in the surface grammar of language, (2) the phenomenology of the use of language, (3) pictures or archetypes embedded in language, (4) the model of presentation and solution of problems in the natural sciences, (5) natural cravings and dispositions of reason."[2] Although most of these philosophical temptations fall under the heading of grammatical errors, the distinctions are useful to show the variety of problems Wittgenstein examines. We will discuss each type briefly to provide some background for the subsequent discussion of sin.

To begin with, Wittgenstein frequently points out ways we are misled by superficial analogies in the surface grammar of language. For example, we naturally model substantive predicates on physical substances. At first glance ideas and pains seem to play the same role in sentences like "I have an idea," or "I have a pain," that cupcakes and warts play in sentences like "I have a cupcake," or "I have a wart." We suppose ideas and pains are like physical substances, only they are in the mind like birds in an aviary, so we conclude that when we speak of having ideas and pains we are reporting the existence of a intrinsically private thing that no one else can know. This raises serious problems about the verification and translatability of the meaning of such private objects, problems that were first explored in Plato's *Theaetetus*, gained renewed difficulty with Descartes, and have continued to plague philosophy up to the present.

Wittgenstein suggests that these problems have had their roots in a misleading analogy. Similarities in surface grammar between the way we speak of things in the mind and the way we speak of things in the world lead us to draw further analogies which overlook differences in depth grammar. Ideas and pains are not things in the mind in the same sense that cupcakes and warts are things in the world. Mental things have special uses in our language that are governed by different grammatical rules. Wittgenstein argues that once we pay attention to these differences in grammar, and are not seduced by superficial analogies, many philosophical difficulties will simply disappear.

The second source of temptation has to do with the phenomenology of the use of language. Wittgenstein writes frequently of how attractive it is to suppose that the images and distinct mental phenomena that often accompany the use of particular words, or the understanding of particular formulas, are themselves the meaning of those words, or at least evidence that meaning should ultimately be explained in terms of mental processes. When someone speaks of the color red we usually imagine a red blur or a red thing perhaps loosely associated with feelings of passion or violence, and when someone mentions the name of a close friend we may imagine the friend in a characteristic pose along with a certain warmth or ease of familarity. In doing philosophy, one keeps returning to the way a formula behind a series is "grasped in a flash." Wittgenstein pays a great deal of attention to the difference one feels when merely tracing the outline of a written sentence as opposed to writing with understanding, or the difference between when one is trying to understand a puzzle and the "ah ha" feeling when one recognizes the solution. All such mental phenomena make a deep impression on us. They lead us to suppose that meanings are derived from mental states, and that understanding is a certain mental atmosphere accompanying a mental process. When doing philosophy, Wittgenstein suggests, the phenomenology of our use of language tempts us to put forth explanations that explain nothing and prevent us from noticing much of what our actual use of language does show us.

A third source of philosophical illusion has to do with the attraction of certain pictures which are embedded in the grammar of language. Perhaps the best example Wittgenstein gives of how we can be seduced by a picture occurs in *Philosophical Investigations* when he discusses the *Tractatus* and the way propositions about facts became the model for language in general. He confesses that in the *Tractatus,* "A picture held us captive" (PI, #115).[3] By this he means that he was seduced by one kind of language, the kind of language which represents facts, and that this blinded him to the variety of forms of language. This leads him to remark: "A main cause of philosophical disease—a one-sided diet: one nourishes one's thinking with only one kind of example" (PI, #593).

A fourth source of philosophical problems opens up when philosophers get seduced by the methods and achievements of the natural sciences. The method of induction—where one forms hypotheses of the greatest possible generality about empirical phenomena and then tests these hypotheses by means of controlled empirical experiments—has enjoyed a great success in the natural sciences. Unfortunately, attempts at applying a similar method in philosophy tend to lead to what Wittgenstein considered metaphysical dogmatics, to confusions between empirical and conceptual questions.[4] Theories about concepts are not testable in the same way as theories about empirical phenomena. Furthermore, Wittgenstein suggests that philosophical theories about concepts cannot even be formulated hypothetically in the first place, since such concepts must always be presupposed in the process of formulating the theory. From his early remarks in the *Notebooks* to the *Philosophical Investigations,* he is unwavering in his claim, "We may not advance any kind of theory" (PI, #109). Nevertheless, the success of the scientific method is very impressive and continues to beckon to philosophers like a siren, only to leave them hopelessly lost and shipwrecked when the seas of language start rising.

A fifth, and in Hacker's list the last, source of philosophical problems described by Wittgenstein has to do with the natural inclination of reason to overreach the bounds of language. In Friedrich Waismann's "Notes on Talks with Wittgenstein," Wittgenstein says that "man has an urge to thrust against the limits of language."[5] We have a tendency to talk of God, of ethical and aesthetic values, and of the meaning of life. While Wittgenstein believes this tendency is absolutely hopeless, he feels that "it is a document of a tendency in the human mind which I personally cannot help respecting deeply and I would not for my life ridicule it" (LE, p. 12). He makes a similar point when he tells Drury that some of the great metaphysical systems of the past are among the noblest productions of the human mind.[6] There is something important and quintessentially human about our drive to say what cannot be said, but it remains, in Wittgenstein's eyes, an endless source of error and, hence, a tendency to be resisted.

Hacker thematically chooses to call the different sources of philosophical problems discussed by Wittgenstein "sources of illusions." Indeed, many of the sources of problems sketched above can easily be construed along Greek lines as riddles and deceptions that require cleverness and resourcefulness to unravel, rather than being construed along Judeo-Christian lines as temptations that require determination of the will. Perhaps the most famous expression of what one could call the "Greek" model of Wittgenstein's philosophical intentions is the remark: "What is your aim in philosophy?—To show the fly the way out of the fly-bottle" (PI, #309). The problem here is ultimately illusory, though it hardly requires the cleverness of Theseus to find the way out of such a simple labyrinth. The fly frantically tries to get out by bumping against the walls of the bottle, a solution which is absolutely hopeless, when the way out of the fly's predicament is readily available from the beginning— all the fly has to do is to leave through the mouth of the bottle.

This way of putting the matter seems to trivialize the philosophical problems, and it naturally leads Gilbert Ryle to ask: "What has a fly lost, who never got into a fly bottle?"[7] If philosophy only rids us of philosophical problems, then it is only of use to philosophers, or in Kenny's words, "Do not get as far as the problems and then you will not need the answers!"[8] The fly in the fly bottle metaphor seems to imply that philosophical problems are arcane scholastic preoccupations that have nothing to do with the cares and concerns of normal human life—after all, only flies get caught in fly bottles.

Although Wittgenstein does occasionally speak of philosophical problems as illusions,[9] such ways of speaking are few compared to his tendency to speak of a perverse will. He constantly shows he is aware of a tension between the right understanding and what we *want* to see. Characteristic phrases like,

"Here we want to say," "We are tempted to say," or "We feel as if " appear on nearly every page. For this reason I believe that the sources of "illusions" enumerated by Hacker are more aptly described as sources of philosophical "temptations."

Part of the inadequacy of speaking of philosophical problems solely in terms of illusions is that it obscures the responsibility of the deceived persons, a responsibility Wittgenstein clearly gives us. In the Judæo-Christian tradition, illusions are usually perpetuated by external forces without an active compliance of the deceived, who are then usually considered morally blameless victims. Speaking of the sources of philosophical problems in terms of temptations puts the moral responsibility more on the tempted individuals. While temptations, like illusions, are thrust upon us, it requires a degree of compliance on our part to make temptations into actual transgressions. St. Paul promises that "God will not tempt us beyond what we can bear."[10] This is not a promise that we will not give in to temptation, but rather it should be taken as a remark about the grammar of "temptation"—namely, that temptations refer to errors that *can* be resisted. Such errors are not believed to have causal control over us, but to influence us through their attractiveness, to seduce us. Giving in to a temptation implies our willing consent to a transgression. When we do philosophy, in Wittgenstein's view, the right understanding is available along with the temptation—we mastered the grammar of our language when we learned to speak—so we are ultimately responsible for resisting the temptation and for seeing the world aright.

One result of describing God as the "fearful judge" is that it frames the character of the world and our place in it. It suggests a world where something important is required of us, where there are standards thrust upon us by which we are judged. Wittgenstein expresses these standards first in terms of logical form and later in terms of logical grammar, but in both cases that which allows for the possibility of complete clarity has a deep and powerful claim on us. In order to insure a one-step hermeneutic, Wittgenstein describes a world in which the rules that prescribe the use of meaningful expressions are sharply defined in terms of a preexisting horizon. Rules, unfortunately, are like double-edged swords, and as biblical writers frequently observed, the same Law which sustains us also condemns us. Once the dictates of logical grammar are compared to the will of God, the stakes are raised to a level where we come face to face with the specter of sin.

Aquinas defines sin as "a word, act, or desire that is against the eternal law."[11] To speak of sin is to suggest a failing more serious than a mere mistake or error due to ignorance or a finite understanding. Sin does not generally include things like miscalculations, misunderstandings and other errors due to human stupidity. Rather, it implies a transgression of something fundamental, something so deep that its claim upon us is indubitable, beyond question. In *The Encyclopedia of Religion,* it is stated that "it is only when the fault is put in the context of a covenantal relation with God that one can speak, *sensu stricto,* of sin (against an expressed divine will)."[12] Sins are not committed because the will of God is unclear. Unlike in the Greek tradition—where what one does not know can bring about one's destruction, as in the story of Oedipus, or where a failure to interpret an ambiguous oracle correctly can destroy a kingdom,[13] or where the forces of the cosmos operate behind a veil and human fortunes depend largely on the wheel of fate, chance, and trickery (consider the *Iliad*)—in the Judeo-Christian tradition nothing important is left to chance or weak understanding, and one is rarely undone from ignorance or the operation of unknown forces. Beginning with Adam and Eve what God required was never hidden or obscure. What he did not command in a clear voice he carved in stone, and when he did resort to speaking through dreams he always provided a reliable interpreter. How then is it possible for us to fail to do what is so obviously required of us? It must not simply be a matter of our failure to solve a riddle or dispel an illusion. Our transgressions can only be the result of a kind of perversity, where something is said, done, or desired in open defiance of the will of God.

According to Wittgenstein, as I understand him, the confusions which characterize philosophical problems are usually of this kind. On the one hand, the dictates of logical grammar are unambiguous and in plain view, and on the other hand, they are still very difficult to accept. Wittgenstein writes:

> If it is asked: "How do sentences manage to represent?"—the answer might be: "Don't you know? You certainly see it, when you use them." For nothing is concealed.
> How do sentences do it?—Don't you know? For nothing is hidden.
> But given this answer: "But you know how sentences do it, for nothing is concealed" one would like to retort "Yes, but it all goes by so quick, and I should like to see it as it were laid open to view."
> Here it is easy to get into that dead-end in philosophy, where one believes that the difficulty of the task consists in our having to describe phenomena that are hard to get hold of, the present experience that slips quickly by, or something of the kind. (PI, #435–#436)

The temptation is to suppose that we could solve what puzzles us if we could only develop a method or apparatus that would allow us to grasp deep and elusive phenomena. In an earlier remark Wittgenstein makes a similar point:

Here it is difficult as it were to keep our heads up,—to see that we must stick to the subjects of our every-day thinking, and not go astray and imagine that we have to describe extreme subtleties, which in turn we are after all quite unable to describe with the means at our disposal. We feel as if we had to repair a torn spider's web with our fingers. (PI, #106)

It is important to note that Wittgenstein is describing a temptation that he himself continued to feel very deeply. In reading his works one frequently feels that he is still trying to repair a torn spider's web with his fingers. But at the same time he rarely loses sight of the fact that this is a dead end, a temptation to be avoided, and he constantly reminds us that the dictates of logical grammar, like the will of God, must be accessible to all. This is why he insists: "Philosophy simply puts everything before us, and neither explains nor deduces anything.—Since everything lies open to view there is nothing to explain. For what is hidden, for example, is of no interest to us" (PI, #126). For Wittgenstein, nothing of ultimate importance could require special skills or cunning. Our salvation cannot depend on the scrupulosity of engineers or the erudition of scholars.

It is widely reported that Wittgenstein was fond of the writings of Tolstoy, but of special relevance here is Drury's report of Wittgenstein's particular fondness for Tolstoy's short tale entitled "The Three Hermits."[14] In this tale Tolstoy tells of a learned bishop who hears of three old hermits living for the salvation of their souls on a secluded island. The bishop seeks out the hermits and discovers that the only prayer they know—"Three are ye, three are we, have mercy upon us!"—indicates only a rudimentary knowledge of the idea of the Holy Trinity and shows great ignorance of the rest of Christian doctrine. So the bishop proceeds to teach them the Lord's Prayer, and with much difficulty the three old hermits manage to learn the prayer by repeating it over and over again to themselves. So the bishop is satisfied, takes his leave and returns to his ship. Then in the middle of the night as the ship sails briskly on its way, the bishop sees something white speeding over the waves after them. Soon he realizes it is the three hermits gliding swiftly upon the water as though they were running over dry land. When they overtake the ship, they tell the bishop that they could no longer remember his teaching and they ask to be taught again. The bishop crosses himself and declares with a newfound humility and some trepidation: "Your own prayer will reach the Lord, men of God. It is not for me to teach you. Pray for us sinners."[15]

John King reports that when Wittgenstein first recommended that he read Tolstoy's *Twenty-Three Tales*, he especially marked four of them—of which

"The Three Hermits" later turned out to be his favorite—and declared, "There you have the essence of Christianity."[16] Part of the attraction of this story for Wittgenstein is indubitably related to the point that when it comes to knowing and doing what is really important—what is, as it were, the will of God—great learning can be of no avail and may even be an impediment. This should not simply be dismissed as a mere symptom of Wittgenstein's prejudice against intellectuals and the academic life. Rather it should be seen as a reflection of his participation in a particular Judeo-Christian religious tradition which holds that what is most fundamental to our salvation cannot be the private possession of experts and cannot require special training. The means to our salvation must somehow be already available to us all, regardless of status, wealth, or education.

Wittgenstein's notion that what we really need to know about logic must already be generally known—that it cannot depend on a special skill, training, or investigation of the world—is a theme that can be traced back to his earliest writings. He insists repeatedly in the *Notebooks* that "logic must take care of itself" (NB, pp. 2, 11). While it is true that in the *Tractatus* he argues that our everyday language disguises our thought (TLP, 4.002) and that analysis could reveal the hidden logical structure, he is emphatic that such sentences do not await analysis by logicians to acquire their senses. In other words, the sentences of everyday language are in perfect logical order just as they stand (TLP, 5.5563), and Wittgenstein's task is just to examine the conditions for the possibility of this order. In this reading, the commitment to perspicuity, to the availability of a clear and unambiguous sense, has priority for Wittgenstein, and the notions of analysis and atomic simples are secondary commitments which are adopted in an attempt to make sense of the possibility of an absolute clarity of logical form. This is supported by the fact that in the *Investigations* Wittgenstein drops the notions of analysis and atomism and adopts other more sophisticated means to the same end. He is still trying to account for the possibility of an absolute clarity of logical form.

In both the *Tractatus* and the *Investigations* Wittgenstein seeks to show how the conditions for a one-step hermeneutic are provided—how the dictates of logic are right before our eyes and how a reliable mode of interpretation, a fixed horizon, is given. This leads us to the question which has continually haunted the Judeo-Christian tradition: if what is required of us is in plain view, then how is it that we allow ourselves to be led astray? The problem cannot simply be a matter of making a careless mistake or an oversight due to limited intelligence or a lack of careful study. On this question

Anthony Kenny quotes a passage from the unpublished manuscript known as the Big Typescript, where Wittgenstein quotes and comments on a remark Tolstoy makes about aesthetics:

> Tolstoy: "The significance of an object lies in its universal intelligibility." That is partly true, partly false. When an object is significant and important what makes it difficult to understand is not the lack of some special instruction in abstruse matters necessary for its understanding, but the conflict between the right understanding of the object and what most men *want* to see. This can make the most obvious things the most difficult to understand. What has to be overcome is not a difficulty of the understanding, but of the will. (MS, 213, 406–407)[17]

On the one hand, Wittgenstein believes Tolstoy is right to insist that the significance of an object lies in something like "its universal intelligibility." This is roughly parallel to Wittgenstein's own refrain, "Don't you know? For nothing is hidden," or the theme in *On Certainty:* "There is something universal here; not just something personal" (OC, #440).[18] On a fundamental level we have to already agree as to the significance and importance of an object or it cannot make an appearance in language at all: "If language is to be a means of communication there must be agreement not only in definitions but also (queer as this may sound) in judgments" (PI, #242). On the other hand, Wittgenstein believes Tolstoy's description of the significance of an object is inadequate, since it fails to account for the difficulty we have in accepting that correct understanding which is known to us all. It is precisely in light of the "universal intelligibility" of important objects that the difficulty we have in understanding them cannot be dismissed as "the lack of some special instruction in abstruse matters." The difficulty can only arise from our perverse will, from the difference between the right understanding and what we want to see.

This brings us back to Wittgenstein's claim that "what has to be overcome is not a difficulty of the understanding, but of the will." When we do philosophy we are continually running into temptations where we have to resist saying and thinking what we want to say and think. In the *Investigations* he writes:

> Consider for example the proceedings that we call "games." I mean board-games, card-games, ball-games, Olympic games, and so on. What is common to them all?— Don't say: "There *must* be something common, or they would not be called 'games'"— but *look and see* whether there is anything common to all. (PI, #66)

To hold to the availability of grammar implies that the wealth of differences between the various proceedings we call "games" are already well known to anyone who has learned our language. Wittgenstein chastises us because we should know better than to insist that there must be something common to everything we call "games"; after all, it is our language, the one we already speak, that we are considering.

It is in light of this theme that we should understand Wittgenstein's often quoted and disparaging remark: "When we do philosophy we are like savages, primitive people, who hear the expressions of civilized men, put a false interpretation on them, and then draw the queerest conclusions from it" (PI, #194). The reproach behind this analogy is not simply that we are inclined to misinterpret things, though we are, but that this inclination is not really a function of ignorance. When we do philosophy we are not, as a matter of fact, looking in from outside at the expressions of a foreign language and culture—like savages hearing the expressions of civilized men—but rather we are native speakers who have no such excuse. The problem is to get us to own up to our own grammar.

Here it should be observed that Wittgenstein speaks of "philosophy" in two very different senses. First, there is the kind of philosophy we have done and are still inclined to do, where "we are like savages" and become seduced by things like overextended grammatical analogies, misleading phenomenal experiences, a priori logical pictures, and inappropriate scientific methods.[19] And then there is the kind of philosophy we ought to do, which respects the expressions "of civilized men." This is the new kind of philosophy Wittgenstein speaks of: "In philosophy we do not draw conclusions. 'But it must be like this!' is not a philosophical proposition. Philosophy only states what everyone admits" (PI, #599).

Wittgenstein sometimes speaks of the new kind of philosophy, his own kind of philosophy, as a matter of replacing metaphysical explanations with grammatical descriptions. The positive implications of giving descriptions will be examined later in chapter 5. Here I just want to draw attention to the negative role of giving descriptions. According to Wittgenstein,

this description gets its light, that is to say its purpose, from the philosophical problems. These are, of course, not empirical problems; they are solved, rather, by looking into the workings of our language, and that in such a way as to make us recognize those workings: *in despite of* an urge to misunderstand them. (PI, #109)

The point is simply to rid ourselves of certain philosophical temptations. The only things that give Wittgenstein's investigation its purpose and significance are the philosophical problems. In this sense, philosophy is indeed nothing more than philosophical problems and their removal. This is an important theme in Wittgenstein's writings, and although it seems to justify the notion that philosophical problems are nothing but illusions, it also justifies other metaphors that have very different implications. For example, it also justifies calling the philosophical problems "a sickness," where the old philosophy is related to the new philosophy like an illness to its cure (PI, #255).

In spite of Wittgenstein's use of a number of metaphors for philosophical problems which imply that the problems are frivolous or trivial, I have suggested that he ultimately believes that there is something about them which is serious and important. On one hand, Wittgenstein claims that these problems are "nothing but houses of cards" (PI, #118),[20] and on the other hand he insists:

The problems arising through a misinterpretation of our forms of language have the character of *depth*. They are deep disquietudes; their roots are as deep in us as the forms of our language and their significance is as great as the importance of our language. (PI, #47)

The discrepancy in Wittgenstein's thinking between philosophical problems not having any proper substance on the one hand, but still having depth and importance on the other hand, seems to arise from his notion that what makes philosophical problems significant is not that they are weighty in themselves, but that they have a powerful hold on human beings.

Against the trivializing suggestion that if philosophy only rids us of philosophical problems then it is only of use to philosophers, Kenny points out a passage in the unpublished manuscripts where Wittgenstein remarks that "philosophy is a tool which is useful only against philosophers and the philosopher in us" (MS, 219, #11).[21] Kenny goes on to suggest that Wittgenstein considered philosophy an unavoidable part of the human condition,[22] and that philosophical problems infest the world "like original sin."[23] This is a powerful and troubling image. The idea that the sins of the parents are visited upon their children has become foreign and repugnant to most of us—it goes against both our laws and our sense of justice.

However, as Kolakowski points out, original sin is not simply a matter of being mysteriously blamed now for something Adam and Eve did long ago, but rather a matter of recognizing our continuing complicity in their act of disobedience and alienation.[24] This is why in Wittgenstein's lectures, he tried to show that "you had confusions you never thought you could have had."[25] We may not be born with false grammatical analogies and misleading pictures, but we do take them in with language. Wittgenstein pursues these latent philosophical problems with all the fierceness and confidence of St. Augustine probing the sins of his infancy in his *Confessions*. When Augustine asks, "What, then, was my sin? Was it that I cried for more as I hung upon the breast?"[26] he wants to impress upon us the depth and breadth of our own sins. In this spirit, Wittgenstein would press his students and would not be satisfied until they recognized problems underlying their own way of speaking and became genuinely bothered by them. The idea that some of his students were not yet infected by philosophical problems is no more considered than Augustine would consider whether or not he had sin as an infant.

Wittgenstein wants to make sure his students dredge through the philosophical problems with him partly because he believes the problems are subtle and pervasive, the sickness is deep, but also because he believes that the problems have a kind of value and importance on their own terms. In some sense, experiencing these problems gives one what used to be called "the fear of God," a thorough sense of dread and awe. Wittgenstein seems to ascribe a positive value to knowing the sordidness and depths of one's sins quite apart from any role this might have in being rid of them. In spite of Wittgenstein's admiration for the simple working life and his claim, "I am by no means sure that I should prefer a continuation of my work by others to a change in the way people live which would make all these questions superfluous" (OC, p. 61), he seems to have more respect for someone who is seriously enmeshed and bothered by metaphysical difficulties, than for those who were never bothered at all. One gets the impression that it is somehow better to undergo a prolonged spiritual struggle in the pursuit of righteousness, than to follow Aristotle's ideal and to do good spontaneously out of habit.

In these attitudes Wittgenstein shows a deep ambivalence toward doing philosophy. Although he often speaks of philosophy as a disease one should rather not have, on some level he seems to believe that it is noble vice and one is in some sense better for it.[27] While it is obviously blameworthy to give in to temptation, Wittgenstein seems to buy into the Judeo-Christian notion that it is a badge of honor to suffer the temptation in the first place. Temptations are especially directed toward those who are "walking with God"— Adam and Eve, Job, King David, Isaiah, Jesus of Nazareth, etc. Apart from the fall, we usually associate temptation stories with individuals of great religious stature—like prophets and saints—who are standing alone, facing the prince of darkness, in a time of anguish and decision. If philosophical problems infest the world like original sin, then when we do philosophy we are putting ourselves in that venerable equivalent to the heroic tradition. For

Wittgenstein, an intense struggle with philosophical temptations shows a spiritual depth of character.

The similarity between the place and shape of sin in Wittgenstein's writings and its place and shape in St. Augustine is illuminating and worth exploring further. On one hand, throughout his *Confessions* Augustine tries to show the depth, breadth and foulness of sin. He traces the most innocuous-looking deeds back to sinful motives, and even seemingly well intended deeds—like his parents' decision to give him a good education—are analyzed in terms of sin. Yet on the other hand, he is emphatic that evil has no substance—a contention he justifies through appropriating a kind of Platonism which views everything, including the death of his close friend and all of his willful wanderings, as being used by God to bring about his eventual salvation. Viewed in this way, God reigns absolute over the world and our problems are ultimately just houses of cards. Evil has no independent substance and sin is self-induced. Given Augustine's Neo-platonic ontology, things appear to be evil because of our blindness to how everything ultimately testifies to the glory of God. But, as with Wittgenstein, this blindness is not caused by mere ignorance, but by a perverse will that knows the good but prefers lower things. The distinctive status of philosophical problems for Wittgenstein is similar to the status of evil and sin for Augustine—although they have no place in the ultimate, God-given scheme of things, they take on tremendous importance because they represent the perversity of the human will.

One can distinguish between two basic ways of viewing sin. Sin can be understood in terms of individual acts, in which case one would normally speak of "sins" in the plural as isolated events or defects in a character that is naturally good. Or sin can be understood as a disposition, a problem of the will, in which case one would normally speak of "sin" in the singular, since everything one does is tainted and the actual acts are uncountable. Sins as isolated acts or desires can be further analyzed into things like pride, lust, envy, etc., and they can be enumerated and confessed. But when sin is seen as a corruption of one's very character, it is superficial and vain to try to enumerate one's errors. One must reach in deeper and address an urge—a perverse will that infects one's entire life. A proper confession of sin in this sense must not merely list one's sins but must, following St. Augustine, tell the *story* of one's sin. One needs to recognize the underlying unity of sin, to grasp the root of a problem which infects one's life as a whole.

It is sin in the singular, a will bent on doing what is forbidden, that Wittgenstein faces with the recognition that "we cannot express what we want to express" (LE, p. 11). In this light we can return to the remark quoted earlier:

The problems arising through a misinterpretation of our forms of language have the character of *depth*. They are deep disquietudes; their roots are as deep in us as the forms of our language and their significance is as great as the importance of our language. (PI, #47)

When Wittgenstein says the significance of these problems is as great as the importance of our language, he seems to be alluding to a point he made in the "Lecture on Ethics," where he compares the question, "Why is there something rather than nothing?" to the question of the existence of language itself (LE, p. 11). The existence of language itself is a paradigm of arbitrariness which cuts right to the heart of religious dependence. At another point he says, "What men mean when they say that 'The world is there' lies close to my heart."[28] All of these questions and remarks are self-referential—they try to express things that are presupposed as a condition of their very expression—but in a deep way that points to our utter dependence on matters of absolute value, our dependence on the will of God. In these cases, we are thrown back to the point that we cannot say what we really want to say. Wanting to go beyond the world, beyond significant language, is a form of excessive pride or willfulness, a failure to trust and have faith in that which both limits and sustains us.

It is important to note that on this level, routine mistakes are not the problem. To make a mistake involves acceptance of an appropriate standard, so mistakes serve to confirm corresponding rules. In the same way, Wittgenstein's repeated admission that "of course, there are borderline cases" is not an admission of any general failure of the rules. On the contrary, it is only because the rules generally hold fast that one can speak of borderline cases at all. The conclusion Wittgenstein draws from such considerations is simple and deliberately restrained: "We have here a *normal* case, and abnormal cases" (PI, #141). The strategy of always admitting the existence of intermediate cases is akin to fighting a forest fire by lighting back fires. By pointing out peculiar cases, surrounding the normal case, where we are not sure whether the grammar applies, Wittgenstein aims to forestall those who would argue that the existence of intermediate cases threatens to call the clarity of grammar in general into question. The existence of intermediate cases is no more a threat to logical grammars than the existence of "an abnormal learner's reaction" (PI, #143) is a threat to our method of teaching a series.

The real danger is not occasional mistakes or the existence of intermediate

cases but the utter failure to accept rules, to submit to the requisite or necessary authority, in the first place.[29] In the previous chapter we discussed the
importance of logic in terms of Dostoevsky's maxim, "If there is no God,
then everything is permitted." Wittgenstein raises the same problem in terms
of suicide:

> If suicide is allowed, then everything is allowed. If anything is not allowed, then suicide
> is not allowed. This throws a light on the nature of ethics, for suicide is, so to speak,
> the elementary sin. (NB, p. 91)

Wittgenstein's reasoning here follows directly from his notion that logical, or
grammatical, form stands over against us like the will of God, both limiting
and sustaining us, and that what is required of us is to be fully reconciled to
it. He is not assuming in the present argument that the limitations the world
places upon us are entirely, or even mostly, the will of God. All that is necessary is for there to be one thing that is forbidden, one limitation demanding
respect and acceptance as the will of God; and suicide would not be allowed,
since it would involve an absolute failure to do what is required of us. On
the other hand, if suicide is permitted that could only mean there are no
limitations; nothing is required of us, so "everything is allowed." However,
for Wittgenstein it is important to note that there *are* limitations, a world of
them, beginning with logical form, and in committing suicide a person man-
ages, as it were, to transgress all these limitations at once.

This reading gives some depth to McGuinness's gloss: "At the end of the
Notebooks Wittgenstein says that suicide is the elementary sin, and I think
his thought is that it is the ultimate form of non-acceptance of what happens."[30] John Moran observes that suicide "constitutes the ultimate disobedience" and has a powerfully corrosive affect on authority.[31] The refusal to
accept anything as given is a refusal to accept any limitations, and this involves the height of hubris or willfulness,[32] the human equivalent of the pride
of the Archangel who was thrown out of heaven for refusing to accept the
sovereignty of God.

So far in this chapter we have considered sin in the singular as a problem
of the will, a will which knows what is required but directs itself towards
other things. However, the perversity of the will takes many forms. We have
already considered what is perhaps the purest form of disobedience, suicide,
and have understood it in terms of an excessive pride that denies the authority of the will of God in its entirety. This will remain the most fundamental
sense of sin that shows itself in Wittgenstein's thought, but some further
distinctions can be made. In the remainder of the chapter we will examine

how excessive pride gives way to the sins of sloth and idolatry in Wittgenstein's writings.

By way of transition we can consider the story of the Tower of Babel. In this story there is both an echo of the overweening pride which led to Lucifer's expulsion from heaven and an overture to the confusion that results when language is no longer grounded in a humble acceptance of God-given work in the world. The basic story reads as follows:

And they said, Go to, let us build us a city and a tower, whose top may reach unto heaven; and let us make us a name, lest we be scattered abroad upon the face of the whole earth.

And the Lord came down to see the city and the tower, which the children of men builded.

And the Lord said, Behold, the people is one, and they have all one language; and this they begin to do: and now nothing will be restrained from them, which they have imagined to do.

Go to, let us go down, and there confound their language, that they may not understand one another's speech.

So the Lord scattered them abroad from thence upon the face of all the earth: and they left off to build the city.[33]

The hubris that leads the children of men to try to make a name for themselves, to transcend the world, and to be the means of their own salvation, calls forth the wrath of God. Taking the story as a metaphor for the source of philosophical confusions, one can suggest that in our pride we repeatedly refuse to accept our given horizons, and this refusal separates us from fundamental sustaining powers and thereby undermines language itself.

A major theme in Wittgenstein's writings has to do with the various ways in which words lose their clear sense once they are removed from their natural home and pressed into metaphysical service. In a couple of remarks that are unusually explicit about the role our excessive pride plays in generating useless expressions, Wittgenstein writes:

It is queer: if I say, without any special occasion, "I know"—for example, "I know that I am now sitting in a chair," this statement seems to me unjustified and presumptuous. But if I make the same statement where there is some need for it, then, although I am not a jot more certain of its truth, it seems to me to be perfectly justified and everyday.

In its language-game it is not presumptuous. There, it has no higher position than, simply, the human language-game. For there it has its restricted application.

But as soon as I say this sentence outside its context, it appears in a false light. For then it is as if I wanted to insist that there are things I *know*. God himself can't say anything to me about them. (OC, #553–#554)

When the expression "I know" is used without a clearly restricted application it is reminiscent of the arrogance of those building the Tower of Babel. It seems out of order, unjustified and presumptuous. The resulting confusion is a function of the proud refusal to abide by limitations that ground our expressions within meaningful human activities.

Wittgenstein repeatedly suggests that when philosophers use words philosophically, the words are ungrounded in preexisting uses and customs, and hence they lack the conditions required for sense. While it could be suggested that Wittgenstein is being capricious—that philosophical uses of words could form distinct language-games of their own, and that there could be philosophical work just like there is agricultural work—he would simply reply that the parallel is flawed, and that philosophy does not have any land to till or seeds to sow. His critique here has both a moral and a grammatical point. Doing metaphysics may be work after a fashion, just as building the Tower of Babel was work, but it is work that does not respect the underlying powers which sustain people's lives. It turns us away from our roots. Doing metaphysics is gratuitous in just the way that building a tower reaching to heaven is gratuitous. In both cases the work is useless and vain: it represents our proud refusal to acknowledge our limits and sources of meaning. Although the surface grammar seems in order, the depth grammar is in shambles, and this ultimately leads to a confusion of tongues.[34]

For Wittgenstein, the possibility that language has a clear sense is dependent on our acceptance of a preexisting horizon. The acceptance of logical or grammatical form must be deeper than mere verbal assent. What we accept will never yield complete clarity unless it stands fast by becoming the unquestioned ground for what we do in our lives. In this sense, what is required of us is absolute, and this is what it means for Wittgenstein to speak of doing the will of God. Tolstoy describes a similar dynamic in *A Confession:*

> The life of the world endures by someone's will—by the life of the whole world and by our lives someone fulfils his purpose. To hope to understand the meaning of that will one must first perform it by doing what is wanted of us. But if I will not do what is wanted of me, I shall never understand what is wanted of me, and still less what is wanted of us all and of the whole world.[35]

Tolstoy's general point finds a more specific application in Wittgenstein's remark, "If he calls *that* in doubt—whatever 'doubt' means here—he will never learn this game" (OC, #329). A great many things in our lives must be accepted and done as a matter of course, without question, before their broader significance can be understood. Tolstoy continues:

If a naked, hungry beggar has been taken from the cross-roads, brought into a building belonging to a beautiful establishment, fed, supplied with drink, and obliged to move a handle up and down, evidently, before discussing why he was taken, why he should move the handle, and whether the whole establishment is reasonably arranged—the beggar should first of all move the handle. If he moves the handle he will understand that it works a pump, that the pump draws water and that the water irrigates the garden beds; then he will be taken from the pumping station to another place where he will gather fruits and will enter into the joy of his master, and, passing from lower to higher work, will understand more of the arrangements of the establishment, and taking part in it will certainly not reproach the master.[36]

When we do metaphysics we are like the hypothetical beggar in Tolstoy's story who insists on questioning the ways of sustaining powers that he is not in a position to understand, questions that would be self-evident if he would simply do as is required of him. The beggar's questions are clarified not through discussion, but through operating the pump.

In a similar way, the problems of metaphysics can be clarified, not through discussion, but through considering language at work. When we do philosophy we frequently try to reason in the abstract, as if our logic were a logic for a vacuum. This leads Wittgenstein to suggest:

> When philosophers use a word—"knowledge," "being," "object," "I," "proposition," "name"—and try to grasp the essence of the thing, one must always ask oneself: is the word ever actually used in this way in the language-game which is its original home?
> What *we* do is to bring words back from their metaphysical to their everyday use. (PI, #116)

As argued earlier, Wittgenstein's way of speaking of "everyday," or "ordinary," language uses can be very misleading.[37] His idea here is simply that philosophical problems would disappear if philosophers would be careful and only use words in ways that respect their established grammars. In other words, when we submit to a preexisting horizon—by using words against the background of established practices where the appropriate precedents, goals, purposes, and standards are grounded in terms of human activities—words can have a clear sense. When we do philosophy, the meaning of troublesome expressions can often be clarified by viewing them in routine applications, by putting them back to work.

In his biography of Wittgenstein, McGuinness points out, "It is usually by ability or inability to work that Wittgenstein measures happiness and unhappiness."[38] Earlier we considered how Wittgenstein linked happiness to doing the will of God.[39] Taken together, these themes give us a simple equation for the phenomenon Max Weber described as the Protestant work ethic. The connection in Wittgenstein between working and doing the will of God can be illuminated by reviewing Weber's basic argument. Weber suggests that with the rise of the Protestant ethic, ordinary work is raised to "the calling,"[40] to a task set by God. For those who came under the influence of this ethic, Weber explains:

The only way of living acceptably to God was not to surpass worldly morality in monastic asceticism, but solely through the fulfillment of the obligations imposed upon the individual by his position in the world. That was his calling.[41]

With the Reformation, work in a sinful world was no longer seen as a practical compromise with the needs of the flesh, nor, following Aquinas,[42] as a natural activity that was morally neutral. Understanding work in the world as a calling allows for the positive valuation of routine activity in the world, and thereby opens up a means for the layman qua layman to glorify God. The priests have been abolished and each individual must become, as it were, a living sacrifice. Weber writes: "The fulfillment of worldly duties is under all circumstances the only way to live acceptably to God. It and it alone is the will of God, and hence every legitimate calling has exactly the same worth in the sight of God."[43] The choice of vocation is a matter of indifference because the real issue has to do with subjugating one's will, and this in turn becomes a matter of how thoroughly one does whatever is required, how completely one engages in one's work.

Wittgenstein's notion of the incomparability of different language-games is best seen in a similar light. This incomparability does not arise from a protagorean relativism—where man is the measure of all things—but from its negation, from the fact that man is *not* the measure of all things. All language-games being on the same level is a function of the depth of our dependence, a function of the fact that we are never in a position to judge between them. Given human finitude and the perversity of the will, the best an individual can do is to embrace a disciplined life in accordance with logical or grammatical form and to thereby ensure that the engine never idles.[44] Tolstoy recognizes the salvatory nature of routine work in the world:

The consciousness of the error in reasonable knowledge helped me to free myself from the temptation of idle ratiocination. The conviction that knowledge of truth can only be found by living led me to doubt the rightness of my life; but I was saved only by the fact that I was able to tear myself from my exclusiveness and to see the real life of the plain working people, and to understand that it alone is real life. I understood that if I wish to understand life and its meaning, I must live a real life, and—taking the meaning given to life by real humanity and merging myself in that life—verify it.[45]

In a later passage Tolstoy continues this point in more explicitly religious terms when he confesses: "I returned to the belief in that Will which produced me and desires something of me. I returned to the belief that the chief and only aim of my life is to be better, i.e., to live in accord with that Will."[46] In this last passage Tolstoy foreshadows Wittgenstein's remark in the *Notebooks* discussed earlier, where he speaks of his need to be "in agreement with that alien will on which I appear dependent" (NB, p. 26). Taken together, Tolstoy's two passages express the Weberian idea that work can be a means of subjugating one's will and aligning it with the will of God. By living in such a way one can hope to imbue one's life in the world with meaning.

It is important to emphasize that when Weber speaks of a calling as a task set by God, he is not thinking of tasks like those set for Hercules—singular adventures appropriate only for heroes—but of routinized work for Everyman. On one hand this harkens back to the notion that what is required of us as the will of God must somehow be available to us all, and on the other hand it returns us to the point that following a rule can only take place within a custom or institution, and that it would be impossible for only one man to follow a rule and to do so only once in his life (PI, #199). While Camus had something very different in mind when he claimed that one must imagine Sisyphus happy,[47] Wittgenstein could easily have adopted the adage for his own. When Sisyphus is set the eternally recurring task of rolling a stone up a hill, he represents an ideal case of routinized work. He has the ultimate calling. Since Wittgenstein links being happy with "doing the will of God," he seems obliged to agree with Camus that Sisyphus of all people must be happy.

The limitation of this example is that for Wittgenstein work produces meaning not only in a grammatical sense—in terms of a custom or practice—but also in a pragmatic sense. The meaning of an expression, for example, is also linked to its usefulness—to the difference it makes—and in these terms the Sisyphus case fails miserably. For Wittgenstein, utility is obviously not the sole criterion of meaning,[48] but it does seem to have special relevance to the problems afflicting philosophers. In a characteristic remark Wittgenstein says: "The confusions which occupy us arise when language is like an engine idling, not when it is doing work" (PI, #132). Here idleness is not lack of motion, but lack of purpose. Idleness in this sense separates us from sustaining powers and obscures the clarity of what is required of us. In other words, it undermines any serious attachment to what makes meaning possible. When Wittgenstein speaks of an engine idling, he is pointing out the source of a malaise that arises when language—or the language user—is not engaging the world. This malaise can be compared to what has traditionally been called "sloth," a sin that includes a range of problems from indolence to ennui, but that has its roots in the failure to do one's God-given duties in the world.

In a study called *The Seven Deadly Sins: Society and Evil,* Richard Lyman devotes a chapter to a consideration of the history of sloth, its various forms, and its corrosive effects.[51] Lyman traces sloth back to the Latin *acedia,* which he translates as "without care," a sin especially attributed to monks and others committed to a religious life, "wherein they became indifferent to their duties and obligations to God."[50] Vagrius (A.D. 400), one of the earliest interpreters of the seven deadly sins, recognized melancholy *(tristitia)* and *acedia* as particular dangers for the desert fathers who had withdrawn from the demands and distractions of society.[51] While turning away from worldly engagements and the temptations they bring, the religious recluse is especially vulnerable to the sin of sloth in all its manifestations. Isolation breeds inactivity, indolence, and apathy. Physically *acedia* is associated with motionlessness and a languishing of the body, mentally with affectlessness, boredom, sluggishness and rancor. An anonymous fifteenth-century encyclopedia called *Jacob's Hell* suggests sloth is the most fundamental sin, a contention it supports by a story about how the devil comes upon an idle man and is able to lead him through all the other deadly sins.[52] Lyman remarks: "The adage 'idle hands are the devil's workshop' here finds its force: for it is among the idle that Satan goes to work, inducing boredom, enervation of the will, and trouble making."[53]

These same problems plague intellectuals, and especially philosophers. In an important sense, contemplation tends to be escapist, to breed inactivity and indifference to work, and to lead to alienation from others, the world, one's self, and eventually, the ground of meaning itself. Lyman points out that "sloth not only subverts the livelihood of the body, taking no care for its day-to-day provisions, but also slows down the mind, halting its attention to matters of great importance."[54] In an irony Wittgenstein would appreciate, it is the philosophers—those who drop everything to pursue the life of the mind—that end up dull-witted and stupid about what is of vital importance.

Perhaps the aristocracy is prone to suffer the corrosive power of *acedia* even more than monastics and contemplatives. Tolstoy could be speaking for Wittgenstein as well when throughout his *Confession* he laments and rails against what he experienced as the institutionalized sloth of the idle rich class:

It came about that the life of our circle, the rich and learned, not merely became distasteful to me, but lost all meaning in my eyes. All our actions, discussions, science and art, presented itself to me in a new light. I understood that it is all merely self-in-dulgence, and that to find a meaning in it is impossible; while the life of the whole labouring people, the whole of mankind who produce life, appeared to me in its true significance. I understood that *that* is life itself, and that the meaning given to that life is true: and I accepted it.

Far from producing sustenance for all, I did not even produce it for myself. I lived as a parasite, and on asking myself, what is the use of my life? I got the reply: "No use." If the meaning of human life lies in supporting it, how could I—who for thirty years had been engaged not on supporting life but on destroying it in myself and in oth-ers—how could I obtain any other answer than that my life was senseless and evil? . . . It was both senseless and evil.[55]

Tolstoy draws an intimate connection between the uselessness and the mean-inglessness of the life of leisure, and he speaks of an emptiness and self-disgust that moved him from ennui to despair. Lyman observes in general that "lei-sure, like hell, holds out much dread and little hope for all who enter its realm."[56]

Perhaps the most famous and articulate case of *acedia* Lyman considers is Hamlet, who suffers from being both something of a philosopher and an aristocrat. Hamlet's distress over the course of events in Denmark leads to hesitation, inactivity, withdrawal, and a paralyzed will. After being exhorted by the ghost of his father, Hamlet wanders aimlessly, knowing what is re-quired of him, but alternately feeling despair and apathy, making it impos-sible to hold to a clear decision or course of action. In the grip of consuming boredom, he craves stimulation as a temporary release from the weariness of the world. In this vein, I would suggest that Hamlet's use of the traveling players is less an effort to reconfirm information he already knew, than an effort to elicit his own deadened feelings. A similar need is behind much of his abuse of Ophelia. It first leads him to trifle with her feelings, and then to lash out and destroy her, milking a kind of satisfaction and cynical amuse-ment from her incomprehension and suffering.

Hamlet is a paradigm of *acedia* and an illuminating example of what can become of a philosopher. Idleness corrodes an active sense of being in the world, routine goals and purposes come into question, everything seems te-dious and uninteresting, and even special events and activities lose their value. One languishes in indolence and sloth. Lyman suggests that the most profound aspect of this condition is the withdrawal from all forms of com-munal activities and the loss of care and concern for others and oneself.[57] Kierkegaard saw to the end of this road when he called despair "the sickness unto death,"[58] a sickness of which suicide is perhaps the ultimate form. This returns us to the notion that the essence of *acedia* is being "without care," a sin that undermines the seriousness and trust that is the foundation of language at work. In other words, when language "goes on holiday" it does not just go to work somewhere else. It becomes useless, and the speaker degenerates into sloth. To call this a sin is to recognize that it involves a failure to accept and do what is ultimately required of us, a transgression, as it were, of our duties to God.

This raises the question of the relation between nonsense and sin. Although Wittgenstein is not entirely consistent on this point, it is important to recognize that it is generally not "nonsense" per se which constitutes the real transgression. Wittgenstein is usually sensitive, especially in his later work, to the playfulness of language. At one point, he ends a discussion of pain with the conclusion that we only ascribe pain and other sensations to living beings and what resembles living beings, and an interlocutor protests:

"But in a fairy tale the pot too can see and hear!" (Certainly; but it *can* also talk.)
"But the fairy tale only invents what is not the case: it does not talk *nonsense*."—It is not as simple as that. Is it false or nonsensical to say that a pot talks? Have we a clear picture of the circumstances in which we should say of a pot that it talked? (Even a nonsense-poem is not nonsense in the same way as the babbling of a child.) (PI, #282)

Wittgenstein is suggesting that there are different kinds of nonsense and that sometimes the line between being false and being nonsensical is not obvious. However, he also implies that intermediate cases do not threaten the validity of the underlying grammar. We may debate whether or not to call a talking pot nonsense, but that does not mean that we do not have a clear picture of the circumstances in which we would say a person is talking. The meaning of "talking" is not being doubted in general, only in how it applies to a specially constructed case. Here again, abnormal cases depend on the normal case. After Wittgenstein writes that the problems plaguing us are "deep disquietudes" that run as deep as language itself, he raises a rhetorical question: "Let us ask ourselves: why do we feel a grammatical joke to be deep? (And that is what the depth of philosophy is)" (PI, #111). While it is not obvious what Wittgenstein means by this, it would seem that the depth of a grammatical joke consists in the uncanny recognition of the inexorable influence the forms of our language exercise over us. Even when openly playing with logical grammar, fairy tales and nonsense poems still presuppose and reinforce the very rules they seem to be flouting. If this were not the case, then most children's literature would leave children hopelessly confused, when in fact it appears effective in teaching them the rudiments of logical grammar. Perhaps this is why Wittgenstein declares: "Don't *for heaven's sake*, be afraid of talking nonsense! But you must pay attention to your nonsense"

(OC, p. 56). Apparently children do pay attention, and they learn what to trust even when—and perhaps especially when—these things are not all standing fast in the story like they should be. In other words, some kinds of nonsense can actually serve to highlight and clarify logical form.[59] In such cases nonsense has nothing to do with sin, because language is still working. Even play is "serious" in Wittgenstein's sense when it is engaged with *care*, when it remains committed to the underlying clarity of grammatical forms.

Wittgenstein suggests that the real problem is not with play or nonsense per se but with disguised nonsense, the kind of nonsense usually produced by philosophers: "My aim is: to teach you to pass from a piece of disguised nonsense to something that is patent nonsense" (PI, #464). In such cases patent nonsense is not simply harmless, but positively therapeutic. Wittgenstein repeatedly takes something we want to say that contains one or another piece of disguised nonsense and replaces it with an analogous situation that is patently absurd. He takes the notion of a private definition—an appeal to a mark or table that exists only in the imagination—and he compares it to buying several copies of the morning paper to assure oneself that what it said was true (PI, #265). The use of private criteria is later compared to having the right hand give the left hand money (PI, #268), and the seductive notion that we know a color by pointing inward at a color sensation is compared to the following: "Imagine someone saying: 'But I know how tall I am!' and laying his hand on top of his head to prove it'" (PI, #279). In each of these cases Wittgenstein takes something we are tempted to say that is disguised nonsense and converts it into something that is patent nonsense, and in this way he hopes to diminish the attraction of the original temptation.

Here again Wittgenstein is addressing the perversity of the will. In the above examples, our attraction to private definitions and private criteria is rooted in our urge to seize necessity by the throat and to secure our own salvation, an urge that reflects a kind of hubris or arrogance that refuses to accept and trust the fundamental forces that limit and support us. In conclusion, the real transgression arises not with "patent nonsense," which can have an honest and legitimate place within human activity, but with "disguised nonsense"—nonsense which is uttered with the presumption that it has a kind of meaning that it is, in fact, incapable of having.

It is just this kind of presumption, a presumption which attributes an ultimate meaning or power to a thing which is incapable of bearing such a meaning or power, that brings us to the sin of idolatry. In the "Big Transcript" Wittgenstein expresses the purpose of his work as follows: "All that philoso-

phy can do is to destroy idols. And that means not making any new ones—
say of 'the absence of idols'" (MS, 213, 413).[60] Idolatry is usually condemned
most sharply where utter submission to the unconditioned sovereignty of the
Deity is most central. In this Wittgenstein shows his Judaic roots, for it is
there, and in some of the Reformed movements in Christianity, that idolatry
is the ultimate sin.

Idolatry aptly describes the form and force of many of Wittgenstein's most
characteristic concerns—from the critiques given in the *Tractatus* of Russell's
theory of types and the idea of "logical objects," to the critiques of essences
and mental images given in the later work. To show the aptness of using the
notion of idolatry to view Wittgenstein's distinctive positions on these philosophical issues, it will be useful to take a brief look at the notion of idolatry
itself. The first law written in the Decalogue reads as follows:

And God spake all these words, saying,
    I am the Lord thy God, which have brought thee out of the land of Egypt, out of the
house of bondage.
    Thou shalt have no other gods before me.
    Thou shalt not make unto thee any graven image, or any likeness of any thing that
is in heaven above, or that is in the earth beneath, or that is in the water under the
earth:
    Thou shalt not bow down thyself to them, nor serve them: for I the Lord thy God
am a jealous God.[61]

In this passage God twice identifies himself as "the Lord thy God," in acknowledgement of his covenant with his chosen people. This is an important
precondition for the sin of idolatry, for it is in contrast to the living God—the
one who has real and ultimate power over us—that idols are defined. God
immediately goes on to give his credentials as the one "which have brought
thee out of the land of Egypt, out of the house of bondage." His deeds are
evidence of his covenant and a reminder of our dependence and obligation.
Perhaps the most striking part of the first commandment is God's thinly
disguised threat at the end: "for I the Lord thy God am a jealous God." It is
in this peculiar and powerful tradition of "a jealous God" that Wittgenstein's
notion of "showing" can best be understood. That which ultimately limits
and sustains us requires our complete faithfulness. Losing a proper sense of
priorities, and putting trust in lesser things, undermines our relationship to
this sustaining power and threatens the ground of meaning itself.

In his *Confessions,* St. Augustine, the adopted father of the Reformed
movement, gives an eloquent and intense account of how idolatry pervaded
his life. Through embracing a Neo-platonic ontology, he is led to understand

the difference between the true God and mere idols as a difference between "the One," as the original and ultimate reality—the end or good from which everything else derives its meaning and being—and "the many," as mere reflections and copies of this reality. In this view, the whole of the physical, social and political world is nothing but imitations and shadows of spiritual reality. Thus Augustine's vast array of worldly loves—insofar as they are loves of things themselves and not of things as they testify to the glory of God—represent his attachment to idols, dispersing his will onto lower things like water onto sand. The fact that these loves continue to have power over him, long after he clearly recognized the need to align his whole will with the will of God, is an endless source of torment and self-condemnation: "In what way, awkwardly and perversely, did I imitate my God? . . . What a sight! A servant running away from his master and following a shadow! What rottenness! What monstrosity of life and what abyss of death!"[62] The later Wittgenstein's critique of essences and his emphasis on the irreducible variety of language-games tend to invert Augustine's Neo-platonic ontology—taking "the many" as the ground of meaning which expresses the will of God and taking the One as an idol which leads us astray—but he still seems to identify with Augustine's intense self-condemnation and sense of misplaced trust. Within their different ontologies, their shared sense of our perverse preference for idols, when the will of God is readily available, is very similar.

The emphatic and enduring prohibition against trying to say what can only be shown, a prohibition we traced from the *Tractatus* to *On Certainty*, can be understood as a sustained effort to overcome idolatry. According to Wittgenstein, questions and issues pertaining to logical or grammatical form cannot be represented, because they involve the method of representation itself and already have to be settled before the question or issue can even be raised. In other words, that which makes sense possible can never lie in the representation or expression itself. James Gustafson's description of idolatry as a problem of "misplaced trust" makes the application to Wittgenstein's philosophical concerns more apparent. Gustafson writes: "Idolatry refers to objects of ultimate trust or confidence that do not and cannot bear the weight of reliance that we place upon them for providing sustenance and meaning."[63] This formulation puts Wittgenstein's injunction against trying "to say what can only be shown" in an appropriate light and gives deeper significance to the seriousness with which Wittgenstein questioned everything from Russell's misplaced trust in "the theory of types" and the substantiality of logical connectives to our misplaced trust in essences and mental images. In what remains of this chapter I will briefly review a number of these issues in terms of Wittgenstein's expressed desire to destroy idols. I do not mean to offer new interpretations of these issues on a technical level, but only to place the accepted readings within a broader ethical/religious framework.

As I have suggested, Wittgenstein's reservations about Russell's theory of types centered not on the correctness of what the theory tried to say, but on the simple fact that Russell tried to *say* it. In 1913 Wittgenstein wrote to Russell: "All theories of types must be done away with by a theory of symbolism showing that what seem to be *different kinds* of things are symbolized by different kinds of symbols, which *cannot* possibly be substituted in one another's places" (NB, p. 121). Hidé Ishiguro's remark on this passage is directly to the point: "Notice here that the right theory is supposed to *show* rather than *say* what we are to understand about symbolism."[64] Whether or not certain signs can be sensibly combined is determined in advance by their logical forms, and logical forms can only be shown. For Wittgenstein, Russell's recourse to the theory of types is not simply extraneous, something to be removed by Ockham's razor, but fundamentally misguided. From the first pages of the *Notebooks 1914–1916*, Wittgenstein was committed to the idea that logic must take care of itself. In the *Tractatus*, the logical form which determines the possible combinations of signs must always already show itself through the use and understanding of any adequate symbolism (including natural languages). Russell's theory of types is an artificial contrivance which leads him away from the ultimate sustaining power he seeks, and in this sense Russell's theory is an idol.

Wittgenstein's contribution to our understanding of the status of relational terms is well known. His doctrine as it appears in the *Tractatus* is brief and without explicit explanation. He writes: "Instead of, 'The complex sign "aRb" says that a stands to b in the relation R,' we ought to put, '*That* "a" stands to "b" in a certain relation says *that* aRb'" (TLP, 3.1432).[65] The point is as elegant as it is simple: in the expression "aRb," the "R" does not correspond to anything in the world. In the paradigm case, "a" and "b" are names that refer to simples, and the expression "aRb" shows how these simples stand to one another. Here the "R" simply means that "a" and "b" are put together in a definite way that models something definite about the way in which the objects they represent are related in the world. In this way, Wittgenstein effectively counters the Platonistic tendency to interpret relations as independently existing entities—entities that he believes do not and cannot bear the weight of reliance that is placed upon them.

Wittgenstein extends this kind of analysis to logical connectives in an effort to get rid of the various kinds of logical objects and logical facts that populate Frege's and Russell's ontologies. Robert Fogelin observes: "It seems natural to treat such binary connectives as conjunction and disjunction as representatives of relations between facts. Viewed this way, these terms serve as names for logical objects. From this it is an easy extension to think of logical truths as pictures of logical facts."[66] Wittgenstein states his objection to thinking of logical constants as objects in many ways, but one of the clearest accounts of his general objection is given in terms of truth tables.

Wittgenstein uses truth tables to display the logical structure of complex propositions in terms of a perspicuous concatenation of elementary propositions. In other words, any nonelementary proposition corresponds to a series of logical operations on elementary propositions and can be completely analyzed in terms of a truth-functional array of elementary propositions. In order to demonstrate that logical constants do not refer to logical objects and that logical truths, or tautologies, do not represent logical facts, Wittgenstein treats the entire truth table as a propositional sign. He gives the following as a basic example:

"p	q		"
T	T	T	
F	T	T	
T	F		
F	F	T	(TLP, 4.442)

Once the order of the truth possibilities of the propositions in the left-hand columns of the schema is preestablished by convention, each different logical operation on the given propositions will correspond to a unique result in the last column. In Wittgenstein's example, the entire truth table can be reduced to "(TTFT)(p,q)," which, assuming the order of truth possibilities given above as standard, corresponds to the familiar expression "p ⊃ q." In this way Wittgenstein has produced a notation that avoids any mention of logical constants, and hence avoids the temptation to suppose that logical constants refer to logical objects. In Wittgenstein's words:

It is clear that a complex of the signs 'F' and 'T' has no object (or complex of objects) corresponding to it, just as there is none corresponding to the horizontal and vertical lines or to the brackets.—There are no 'logical objects.'

Of course the same applies to all signs that express what the schemata of 'T's' and 'F's' express. (TLP, 4.441)

To suppose that there exist "logical objects" behind each of our signs for logical constants, is to attribute a kind of meaning and power to these signs which they cannot bear. For Wittgenstein this is a serious matter of misplaced trust. In the *Tractatus* the world is composed of facts—determinate concatenations of objects—and what sustains logical structure and determines the range of possible facts is nothing other than the internal forms or properties of all the objects. The notion that the signs for logical constants represent distinct logical objects which in turn sustain logical structure, is an error that simply turns the signs into idols.

Frege's assertion sign "⊢" is another piece of logical notation that Wittgenstein considers an object of misplaced trust. Frege uses this symbol to express his doctrine that every proposition contains an "assumption," which is the thing being asserted. According to this doctrine, a proper analysis of a proposition will distinguish the assertoric force from the truth being mentioned. For example, the proposition, "The grass is green," should be analyzed as: "It is asserted that the grass is green." By this means Frege intends to maintain the important distinction between what is asserted and what is true. For the present purposes it is not necessary to give a fuller account of Frege's reasons for this distinction, nor will it be helpful to evaluate the power and justice of Wittgenstein's critique;[67] the purpose here is simply to highlight the shape and nature of Wittgenstein's response and to place it within a larger pattern of ethical and religious issues and concerns.

In a parenthetical remark made during his discussion of truth tables, Wittgenstein declares:

Frege's "judgment-stroke" "⊢" is logically quite meaningless: in the works of Frege (and Russell) it simply indicates that these authors hold the propositions marked with this sign to be true. Thus "⊢" is no more a component part of a proposition than is, for instance, the proposition's number. It is quite impossible for a proposition to state that it itself is true. (TLP, 4.442)[68]

While Wittgenstein thinks Frege is right to want to distinguish between an assertion and the truth, he believes that by introducing a "judgment-stroke" before the assumption Frege has simply produced an artificial and ineffectual device, an idol, which is incapable of doing the work that is required of it.

In other words, Wittgenstein suggests that the distinction between an assertion and the truth must already be integrated into any adequate theory of representation. As matters stand, Frege's assertion sign fails to engage the logic of the proposition and his assumption in effect serves as both the sense and the truth of the assertion. Hence there is no room within the logic of the proposition to distinguish the assertoric force from the truth of the proposition, and Frege is obliged to resort to what Wittgenstein considers a *deus ex machina*. What Frege needs is an internal way to distinguish between sense and truth that still preserves an intimate connection between them. In the *Tractatus* Wittgenstein seeks to accomplish this by his picture theory, which makes a firm distinction between sense and truth—between possible states of affairs and what happens to be the case—while intimately linking them through the identity of pictorial form and logical form. The reason Wittgenstein declares that "it is quite impossible for a proposition to state that it itself is true," is that the identity of pictorial form and logical form, and the correspondence between a picture and the world, can only be shown. As with the theory of types, the assertion sign represents an attempt to say what can only be shown. It represents another misguided appeal to an impotent idol which cannot support the weight of reliance that is placed upon it.

In Wittgenstein's later writings a similar pattern of destroying idols appears. We have already mentioned Wittgenstein's critique of our reliance on essences. This is a crucial theme that pervades his later thought, and more should be said. The most famous passage that addresses this problem I now quote in full:

> Consider for example the proceedings that we call "games." I mean board-games, card-games, ball-games, Olympic games, and so on. What is common to them all?— Don't say: "There *must* be something common, or they would not be called 'games'"— but *look and see* whether there is anything common to all.—For if you look at them you will not see something that is common to *all*, but similarities, relationships, and a whole series of them at that. (PI, #66)

We feel that there must be some thread, an essence, that runs through all the cases of games, but this feeling is an endless source of idols. As long as we grasp for essences we will keep coming up with things that cannot support the weight of reliance that is being placed upon them. None of the similarities or relationships is *essential*—no single thread runs the length of a rope. What makes a rope usable, Wittgenstein suggests, is simply the overlapping of many fibers (PI, #67). In most cases, when we demand an essence for a class of things, we already know it is a misguided and futile quest, but it is so attractive that we find it difficult to resist. In PI #66, for example, Wittgenstein goes on to remind us of a diverse array of games with which we are all well acquainted. Then in the following remark, in order to wean us from our willful pursuit of essences, he introduces the notion of "family resemblances" as a nonidolatrous way to describe how such a loose confederacy can all be called "games."

In the *Philosophical Investigations,* some other examples of objects of trust that cannot bear the weight of reliance that is placed upon them include ostensive definitions, rules, and mental images and processes. In the first two cases Wittgenstein does not deny that they play a part in language, he just attacks our tendency to attribute ultimate power and meaning to what are merely the props and accessories for language. In the latter two cases he does not deny the existence of mental phenomena, but he does suggest that they have no part to play *within* language and that they cannot tell us about the grammar and meaning of words.

The first thing Wittgenstein has to say about ostensive definition is that it already involves a kind of mastery of a particular language-game. In the earliest stages of teaching a language, one may direct a child's attention to various things while uttering the appropriate words, and in regard to this level of training Wittgenstein remarks: "I do not want to call this 'ostensive definition,' because the child cannot as yet *ask* what the name is. I will call it 'ostensive teaching of words'" (PI, #6). At this point one may succeed in establishing an association between a word and a thing, but it is still premature to call these "names," since there are many other kinds of associations between words and things. Even later, after the child has mastered the game of naming, the process of giving ostensive definitions remains a limited gesture that always depends on a host of preestablished conditions to be successful. Wittgenstein writes:

> Now one can ostensively define a proper name, the name of a colour, the name of a material, a numeral, the name of a point of the compass and so on. The definition of the number two, "That is called 'two'"—pointing to two nuts—is perfectly exact.— But how can two be defined like that? The person one gives the definition to doesn't know what one wants to call "two"; he will suppose that "two" is the name given to *this* group of nuts!—He *may* suppose this; but perhaps he does not. He might make the opposite mistake; when I want to assign a name to this group of nuts, he might understand it as a numeral. And he might equally well take the name of a person, of which I give an ostensive definition, as that of a colour, of a race, or even of a point of the compass. That is to say: an ostensive definition can be variously interpreted in *every* case. (PI, #28)

In the normal course of events, however, ostensive definitions are a perfectly adequate means of communication. When Wittgenstein concludes that they can be variously interpreted, the point is only that there is nothing in an ostensive definition itself which establishes the connection between a word and a meaning. Sometimes misunderstandings may be averted in particular cases by making the definitions more specific—for example, saying, "This *number* is called two," or "This *color* is called sepia," etc.—but this only pushes the problem of interpretation to another level. One still needs to define "number" and "color." Whether further specification will avert a misunderstanding will depend on a whole set of additional circumstances—including the person with whom one is speaking and the presence of preestablished customs surrounding its use. Ultimately, what makes ostensive definition successful does not lie in the definition itself but in the given form of life—the network of preexisting conditions—that govern its employment.

Wittgenstein makes a similar analysis of rule following. During an extensive discussion of what it means to follow a rule, he writes:

> "But this initial segment of a series obviously admitted of various interpretations (e.g. by algebraic expressions) and so you must first have chosen *one* such interpretation."—Not at all. A doubt was possible in certain circumstances. But that is not to say that I did doubt, or even could doubt. . . .
>
> So it must have been intuition that removed this doubt?—If intuition is an inner voice—how do I know *how* I am to obey it? And if it can guide me right, it can also guide me wrong. (PI, #213)

Again, the point is not that rules are inadequate to their purpose, but rather that they are insufficient by themselves—a rule cannot give its own application. There must be something apart from the rules themselves which governs their use and grounds "a way of grasping a rule which is *not* an *interpretation,* but which is exhibited in what we call 'obeying the rule' and 'going against it' in actual cases" (PI, #201).

The precondition for the possibility of following a rule is that it must be enacted within a language-game or form of life which governs its application. In other words, rule following can only take place against a background of preexisting customs, uses and institutions (PI, #199). This is why, in order to be initiated into the use of rules, the rules themselves are never enough. Wittgenstein writes: "Not only rules, but also examples are needed for establishing a practice. Our rules leave loopholes open, and the practice has to speak for itself" (OC, #139). Wittgenstein means to question the idea that the loopholes can be plugged by simply resorting to further rules, just as he also doubts that an ostensive definition can be clarified by simply increasing the specificity of the definition. Although misunderstandings may sometimes be averted by such means, no number of rules or definitions can force someone to accept a particular interpretation or to attach the correct meaning to a thing. In order to avoid turning rules and definitions into idols, Wittgenstein feels it is imperative to eliminate our misplaced trusts and to acknowledge from the start what really has the power to ground meaning.

Wittgenstein's discussion of the inadequacy of appealing to mental images and processes when trying to understand meaning is closely related to his discussion of ostensive definition and rule following. When trying to isolate the exact meaning of the word "red," for example, one is tempted to point inwardly to the mental image that appears before one's mind when one says or thinks that something is red. This not only raises the problem associated with giving ostensive definitions—namely that the image may be variously interpreted in every case,—but it also raises the question of the relation between logical grammar and "private" psychological phenomena. Just what does a mental image of a thing have to do with the meaning of a thing? One strategy Wittgenstein adopts is to see if it makes any difference to imagine them unhinged:

> "Imagine a person whose memory could not retain *what* the word 'pain' meant—so that he constantly called different things by that name—but nevertheless used the word in a way fitting in with the usual symptoms and presuppositions of pain"—in short he uses it as we all do. Here I should like to say: a wheel that can be turned though nothing else moves with it, is not part of the mechanism.
>
> The essential thing about private experience is really not that each person possesses his own exemplar, but that nobody knows whether other people also have *this* or something else. The assumption would thus be possible—though unverifiable—that one section of mankind had one sensation of red and another section another. (PI, #271–#272)[69]

To suppose that meaning must reside in a mental image is a seductive notion, and it can be seen as a semantic equivalent of the temptation which overcame the twelve tribes of Israel while they were waiting for Moses to come down from Mount Sinai. They had just been delivered out of Egypt, and they could not resist the idea that the ultimate power which had and would continue to sustain them must reside in a graven image. So they lost faith in the unseen God and his absent servant Moses, and they made themselves a golden image of a calf. The images produced in the mind may strike us with great force and vivacity, but according to Wittgenstein they are as incapable of sustaining meaning as the golden calf was incapable of delivering and sustaining the children of Israel.

In these remarks, Wittgenstein is not denying that mental images frequently accompany our use of certain words or that mental processes occur when we think or say meaningful things. He is simply suggesting that mental images and sensations are not part of language, even when they appear to be the intended object, and that mental processes can be separated from questions of logical grammar and meaning. Wittgenstein writes:

"But you surely cannot deny that, for example, in remembering, an inner process takes place."—What gives the impression that we want to deny anything? When one says "Still, an inner process does take place here"—one wants to go on: "After all, you *see* it." And it is this inner process that one means by the word "remembering."—The impression that we wanted to deny something arises from our setting our faces against the picture of the 'inner process.' What we deny is that the picture of the inner process gives us the correct idea of the use of the word "to remember." We say that this picture with its ramifications stands in the way of our seeing the use of the word as it is. (PI, #305)

Our obsession with the picture of the inner process obscures our view of the logical grammar which actually sustains the meaning of our words. Mental phenomena may indeed accompany our use of words, but to suppose they represent the meaning of these words involves the same kind of perversity as that of the slave mentioned by St. Augustine who abandoned his master and went off chasing his master's shadow.

We have suggested that Wittgenstein's intense efforts to sweep away extraneous or gratuitous appeals to logical objects, assertion signs, ostensive definitions, rules, and mental images and processes, cannot be adequately described in terms of an aesthetic or heuristic commitment to honesty and simplicity. He frequently wields Ockham's razor with all the zeal and moral indignation of Jesus clearing the money changers and merchants out of the temple. There is something more at stake in Wittgenstein's work than mere simplicity. As our brief survey of some of the more famous and characteristic themes from the *Tractatus* to the *Philosophical Investigations* has illustrated, Wittgenstein's writings reflect a commitment to destroying idols. He persistently and ingeniously detects and attacks our appeals, in Gustafson's apt words, "to objects of ultimate trust or confidence that do not and cannot bear the weight of reliance that we place upon them for providing sustenance and meaning."[70] The point, of course, is to restore trust in the proper direction. This reading highlights the difference between Wittgenstein's actual work and his largely undeserved reputation for undermining trust per se—a reputation that is rarely championed explicitly but nevertheless seems to lurk in the background, via whispered charges of relativism, whenever Wittgenstein's name appears. Part of the significance of calling something an idol is the implicit acknowledgment of something else that is worthy of our trust and confidence.

Throughout his writings, Wittgenstein endeavors to clarify the limits of language and to demonstrate that the possibility of saying is always dependent on a kind of showing, that the possibility of using language is always dependent on a prior existence of logical form or logical grammar. I have argued that, for Wittgenstein, the say/show distinction comes to take on ethical and religious significance. It comes to represent our more general need to recognize that we are ultimately dependent on preestablished conditions that lie forever beyond our personal control—that we are ultimately dependent, as it were, on the mercy and grace of God.

For Wittgenstein, the say/show distinction also implies that the preestablished conditions that bear down upon and sustain us are ultimately perspicuous and "open to view." They show themselves. They lie before us like the will of God, a will that is never hidden or obscure. So it must not simply be ignorance, stupidity and bad fortune that separate us from the redeeming powers, but the perversity of sin.

In the present chapter, I have considered Wittgenstein's analysis of the impediments and errors that thwart a philosopher's recognition of the ground of meaning, and I have compared them to certain traditional sins, such as pride, sloth and idolatry. The sin of pride is reflected in our willful refusal to accept and abide by the limits of language, limits that are evident to everyone and established by an authority which we may not dispute. Sloth is the sin which describes the meaninglessness and ennui which results when someone is alienated from routine work in the world. This represents a critical failure from the point of view of a semantic system that is based on use within practices and habitual activities—where meaning atrophies when "the engine is idling" or when "language goes on holiday." Idolatry is the sin Wittgenstein addresses when he repeatedly attacks our tendency to create or appeal to objects of ultimate trust which are unable to support the weight of reliance placed in them. In each case, I have placed Wittgenstein's distinctive views on problems in logic and language within an ethical/religious study—a study of the impediments and errors that thwart a proper recognition and trust in that which both limits us and is able to provide sustenance and meaning.

5

WRITING TO THE GLORY OF GOD

In this final chapter I will present a more general discussion of the nature of Wittgenstein's writings and of the distinctive spirit that permeates them. In his preface to the *Philosophical Remarks* Wittgenstein claimed that the spirit in which he is writing "is different from the one which informs the vast stream of European and American civilization in which all of us stand" (PR, p. 7). In a personal remark to M. O'C. Drury he reiterated: "My type of thinking is not wanted in this present age, I have to swim so strongly against the tide."[1] While his sense of being at odds with the times was probably exacerbated both by his particular and demanding personality and by the fact that he lived much of his adult life in foreign countries, it also reflects an important aspect of his writings and takes us to the heart of his way of thinking.

G. H. von Wright is surely on target when he observes that Wittgenstein's "conception of philosophy is intimately allied to a way of viewing contemporary civilization."[2] Wittgenstein considered the spirit of our modern industrial age "alien and uncongenial" (CV, p. 6), and he frequently expressed a strong sense that we are living in dark times.[3] However, it is one thing to see that in an important sense Wittgenstein's writings are against the spirit of our contemporary culture, but it is another thing to see their positive significance. One way to try to orient ourselves to the spirit of Wittgenstein's writings is to imagine an age when these writings would be at home and would be, as it were, the natural expression of a people; but this approach tends to yield conflicting results.

On the one hand, Wittgenstein's way of thinking seems to take its inspiration from an earlier age. J. C. Nyíri suggests that Wittgenstein can be seen in relation to certain currents of conservatism,[4] and indeed Wittgenstein often does identify with aspects of Western culture that had died by 1850.[5] It is not difficult to understand why Wittgenstein includes Spengler among those who had influenced his way of thinking (CV, p. 19). Von Wright points out that "Wittgenstein did not, like Spengler, develop a philosophy of history. But he *lived* the *'Untergang des Abendlandes,'* the decline of the West, one could say. He lived it, not only in his disgust for contemporary Western civilization, but also in his deep awe and understanding of this civilization's great past."[6] This all gives rise to a clear strand of nostalgia in Wittgenstein's writings and makes it seem he is longing for an earlier age.

On the other hand, it is also important to see with Brian McGuinness that Wittgenstein's way of thinking anticipates a radically new age, that he "himself felt that he was writing for a future race, for people who would think in a totally different way."[7] After lamenting to Drury that his type of thinking was not wanted in the present age, he continued: "Perhaps in a hundred years people will really want what I am writing."[8] Wittgenstein emphasizes that in order for a people to think in a different way, they would also have to live in a different way. And this means that thinking in a different way is not something that can be effected through the isolated activity of an individual. Something deeply rooted in the society as a whole needs to change. In the *Remarks on the Foundation of Mathematics,* Wittgenstein suggests:

> The sickness of a time is cured by an alteration in the mode of life of human beings, and it was possible for the sickness of philosophical problems to get cured only through a changed mode of thought and of life, not through a medicine invented by an individual.
> Think of the use of the motor-car producing or encouraging certain sicknesses, and mankind being plagued by such sickness until, from some cause or other, as the result of some development or other, it abandons the habit of driving. (RFM, p. 132)

However, this allusion to the end of the practice of driving motor-cars is simply offered as a metaphor, and as Von Wright observes, Wittgenstein is not a prophet in the traditional sense in that he does not presume to have a clear vision of the future.[9] This lack of foreknowledge is not just a matter of his personal choice or interests. Wittgenstein thinks it is part of the nature of things that the future is inscrutable. At one point in *Culture and Value* he writes, "You can't *build* clouds. And that's why the future you *dream* of never comes true" (CV, p. 41),[10] and later he remarks: "Who knows the laws according to which society develops? I am quite sure they are a closed book even to the cleverest of men" (CV, p. 60).

Ultimately it is misleading to say Wittgenstein's way of thinking belongs either in the past or the future, or even to say that it is backward or forward looking. In a curious way, his philosophical investigations are almost entirely focused on the present. In the *Remarks on the Foundations of Mathematics,* for example, he declares: "Our task is, not to discover calculi, but to describe the *present* situation" (RFM, p. 210). In his writings there is as little attention paid to historical problems and development as to future problems or possible utopias.[11] Rather, he engages in an intense analysis of the standards and failings present in contemporary forms of speech. In other words, he restricts himself to giving a kind of diagnosis which refuses to appeal either to historical causes and explanations or to predictions and prescriptions for the future, considering them all unreliable and ultimately irrelevant. What Wittgenstein seeks in his investigations is always something which is immediately at hand. In *On Certainty* he writes:

> If I say "Of course I know that that's a towel" I am making an *utterance* [*Äußerung*].[12] I have no thought of a verification. For me it is an immediate utterance [*Äußerung*].
> I don't think of past or future. (And of course it's the same for Moore, too.)
> It is just like directly taking hold of something, as I take hold of my towel without having doubts. (OC, #510)

Although this arises in the specific context of Moore-type propositions, it corresponds to an important characteristic of his writings, namely that they focus on what is ready to hand. Wittgenstein is interested in understanding the logical concepts we already possess, not in speculating about the construction of ideal concepts.

In this regard, it is important to note that Wittgenstein consistently finds "hypothetical" considerations irrelevant to doing logical analysis. Hypotheticals have to do with what may or may not be the case. Hypotheses may be appropriate when doing science, where they can be confirmed or falsified by empirical experiments, but the presence of hypotheticals in philosophy, he would suggest, usually indicates a confusion between empirical and conceptual investigations.[13] Consider the following example:

> "I *know* that it never happened, for if it had happened I could not possibly have forgotten it."
> But supposing it *did* happen, then it just would have been the case that you had forgotten it. And how do you know that you could not possibly have forgotten it? Isn't that just from earlier experience? (OC, #224)

Wittgenstein suggests that a claim based on hypothetical considerations is ultimately dependent on the vagaries of experience—a matter for empirical science—whereas logical analysis would have to do with an investigation of existing concepts.

This is a fundamental theme throughout Wittgenstein's writings. In the *Notebooks* he writes, "Remember that there are no hypothetical internal relations" (NB, p. 19)—the point being that internal relations are a reflection of the logical form of objects and hence any *possible* internal relation is already *necessary* from the beginning (TLP, 2.012–2.01231)—and in the *Investigations* he still insists that "there must not be anything hypothetical in our considerations" (PI, #109). In both the early and the later work the irrelevancy of hypothetical considerations is a direct result of his fundamental notion that determinations of logical form, or logical grammar, are utterly dependent on preestablished conditions, whether in terms of the internal form of tractarian objects (TLP, 2.0123–2.0124), or later in terms of preexisting language-games and forms of life. In either case, the thorough acceptance of these given conditions is a prerequisite for doing logic at all.

The argument here involves two premises. First, logic is about necessary connections, and second, hypothetical conditions can be variously interpreted in every case. From these premises it follows that logical connections cannot be derived from hypothetical conditions. The possibility of necessary connections is dependent on our prior and genuine acceptance of certain conditions, an acceptance that shows itself in our mastery of particular skills, procedures or language-games in which certain things follow as a matter of course—"as much as it is a matter of course for me to call this colour 'blue'" (PI, #238). The investigation of logical form, or logical grammar, is tied to the present insofar as it is ultimately predicated on the mastery of certain concepts, on the possession of the appropriate skills indicative of one's actual participation in a form of life.

Some have argued that it does not follow from the fact that interpretations depend on preestablished conditions, that these conditions must be accepted uncritically.[14] In this view, one can often understand things without believing them precisely because it is possible to form valid interpretations based on tentative or hypothetical acceptance of the appropriate preestablished conditions. This is to suggest, in short, that it is possible to play, or at least to be a master of, a language-game while withholding assent. Although this argument has some appeal on its own terms, it seems to miss the central point of Wittgenstein's analysis. If it is true to say that hypothetical conditions can be variously interpreted in every case, and that this means there must be a way of following a rule which is not an interpretation but is a custom one follows as a matter of course, then it is begging the question to speak of playing a language-game while withholding assent. Until certain fundamental things follow as a matter of course, one will simply not be able to play the game.

In spite of his injunction against hypothetical considerations, Wittgenstein himself often posits hypothetical language-games that are played very differently from our own, such as the table which is read across at a diagonal instead of as we normally read (PI, #86), or the finger which points from tip to hand instead of the other way around (PI, #185). However, for Wittgenstein it is crucial to realize that such hypothetical considerations cannot lead to constructive contributions to logic. They are only useful in the treatment of philosophical diseases. Only philosophers and those infected with philosophical ways of thinking, he argues, will have any use for his remarks. His hypothetical language-games have no logical significance in themselves—it is only the philosophical problems which give them their sense and purpose[15]—and healthy minded people should find them nonsensical and pointless. In this sense, "the philosopher's treatment of a question is like the treatment of an illness" (PI, #255), and his own hypothetical language-games are meant to be like medicines which eliminate themselves along with the diseases they treat. In the imagined cases of aberrant table reading and finger pointing mentioned above, the idea is not that in fact "anything goes" but that in theory "anything goes."[16] This is why Wittgenstein wants "to bring words back from their metaphysical to their everyday use" (PI, #116). The clear determinations sought by the logician are dependent on leaving the realm of theory and returning to where there are rules which are followed as a matter of course.

In *On Certainty* Wittgenstein writes: "I really want to say that a language-game is only possible if one trusts something (I did not say 'Can trust something')" (OC, #509), and similar remarks are thematic throughout his later writings. One may find the circularity between understanding and doing (or believing) to be frustrating or philosophically unsatisfying, but it is important to realize that this circularity (whether vicious or virtuous) is fundamental to Wittgenstein's way of thinking. At some point critical distance, or doubt, is incompatible with understanding because understanding requires a level of participation that can only be achieved through submission to a kind of training within a form of life. It is only through this training, not some kind of cognitive introspection, that hermeneutics can avoid a vicious circle—our agreement in judgments can only derive from an agreement in forms of life (PI, #241).

In this sense, for Wittgenstein, being a logician has clear affinities with being religious, and he recognizes this when he confesses to Drury: "I cannot help seeing every problem from a religious point of view."[17] Wittgenstein's point when positing obscure tribes with hypothetical language-games is often reminiscent of Jesus' saying, "You do not believe because you are not sheep of my flock."[18] Leszek Kolakowski writes that "people are initiated into the understanding of a religious language and into worship through participation in the life of a religious community, rather than through rational persuasion,"[19] and the same could be said for how people are initiated into the understanding of logical forms. Earlier Kolakowski quotes the medieval adage *credo ut intelligam* to suggest that in religious matters understanding follows belief.[20] Neither logic nor religious belief can be approached hypothetically, since both are dependent on a prior and genuine commitment that goes deeper than intellectually or cognitively entertaining possibilities. According to Wittgenstein, logic, like religion, is dependent on submitting oneself almost bodily to a kind of training in a form of life.

We began this chapter by considering both Wittgenstein's expressed disgust for our modern industrial civilization and his claim that he is writing in a different spirit. It seemed inadequate to describe this spirit either as a longing for the past or as a longing for the future, and instead I compared it to a kind of religious spirit which recognizes our dependence on what is given and considers hypothetical considerations idle and vain. According to this spirit, the significance of the past and any hope for the future must both somehow be sought in the present, in an immediate apprehension of and participation in those ultimate realities which command our immediate obedience and respect. However, in light of Wittgenstein's profound dependence on and recourse to "what there is," his emphatic efforts to distance himself from his contemporary civilization appear paradoxical. This suggests a more complicated attitude toward the world than mere acceptance or rejection.

Before discussing Wittgenstein's attitude further, it will be useful to try to place him with respect to the schema of worldviews Max Weber develops in his sweeping study of different world religions. Weber classifies the major world religions according to their attitudes toward the world. After distinguishing between those religions that affirm the world, such as Confucianism, and those that reject the world, he makes a further distinction in the latter between a disenchantment with the world which takes the world as ultimately illusory, and one which takes the world as evil or sinful. When the world is taken as illusory, the tendency is to seek to escape by ridding oneself of all desires and attachments to the world, a kind of "otherworldly asceticism" such as is found in Buddhism. And when the world is taken as sinful the tendency is neither simply to abandon nor to accept the world, but to engage in what Weber calls "worldly asceticism," where routine work in the world is encouraged, but for spiritual reasons rather than for worldly benefits. One is encouraged to embrace the discipline of a vocation both to subdue one's willful, sinful nature and to provide a bulwark against the world, a world which is not an illusion but substantial and evil. Worldly asceticism finds a classic expression in the Pauline admonition that the Christian should be "in the world but not of the world." Although, according to Weber, the peculiar disenchantment with the world which leads to worldly asceticism is found in its most virulent form in Calvinist strands of Protestantism, it represents a tendency that runs through the entire Judeo-Christian tradition.[21]

Wittgenstein's writings, I would suggest, should be placed squarely in this tradition. In his denouncement and rejection of the ways of his civilization, he never loses sight of the fact that he remains a product of this civilization and that he cannot simply escape it. In this sense he clearly recognizes the importance of being "in the world but not of the world." When reflecting on the nature and purpose of his writing he observes:

But it is true to say that, in my opinion, this book has nothing to do with the progressive civilization of Europe and America—that this civilization is perhaps the environment essential to the spirit of the book, but that the two have different goals. (MS, 109, 208–209)[22]

No matter how distasteful Wittgenstein found his contemporary culture, his thought remains tied to the present time and to understanding and combating certain sicknesses infecting our given forms of life. This is why he suggests that our worldly civilization is "the environment essential to the spirit of the book." This is much like saying that the decadence and degeneration of Rome is the environment essential to St. Augustine's *City of God.* Although the two cities have very different goals, they are both *in* the world. The "City of God" is not the celestial city waiting for us in the hereafter. It is a city that is designed around the practice of worldly asceticism, a city that is intended to be "in the world but not of the world."

Wittgenstein's attitude toward his times reflects a similar tension. His writings represent a profound disenchantment with a world that cannot be escaped and should not be ignored. Our language is there, thrust upon us, and it is an occasion for both deep respect and dread, even worship and loathing, as though it were both created as a gift from God and infected subsequently with original sin. One must engage it and even embrace it, but with a will that is transformed and resistant to certain prevalent temptations.[23] This, I would suggest, is the key to the striking and enigmatic remark Wittgenstein makes in the foreword to the *Philosophical Remarks:*

I would like to say 'This book is written to the glory of God,' but nowadays that would be chicanery, that is, it would not be rightly understood. It means the book is written in good will, and in so far as it is not so written, but out of vanity, etc., the author would wish to see it condemned. He cannot free it of these impurities further than he himself is free of them. (PR, p. 7)

Later we will return to the question of what it means to write "to the glory of God." For now suffice it to say that in the present age "it would not be rightly understood," and that it has to do with a way of writing, and living, that is not governed by pride, vanity, idolatry, or any of the other sins discussed in the previous chapter.

The general failure of our age to resist these temptations manifests itself in many ways. In the foreword to the *Philosophical Remarks* Wittgenstein mentions our civilization's cancerous obsession with size, with "building ever larger and more complicated structures" (PR, Foreword, p. 7), and elsewhere he objects to its blind and almost mechanical belief in progress,[24] and especially to its pathological presumption that everything can be explained. I will discuss in detail our tendency to demand explanations, since it is a theme that is treated extensively throughout Wittgenstein's writings. His objection to this tendency is already expressed in an often quoted passage from the *Tractatus:*

The whole modern conception of the world is founded on the illusion that the so-called laws of nature are the explanations of natural phenomena.

Thus people today stop at the laws of nature, treating them as something inviolable, just as God and Fate were treated in past ages.

And in fact both are right and both wrong: though the view of the ancients is clearer in so far as they have a clear and acknowledged terminus, while the modern system tries to make it look as if *everything* were explained. (TLP, 6.371; TLP, 6.372)

Wittgenstein considered it important to recognize that "explanations come to an end somewhere" (PI, #1). He felt that our modern industrial civilization is dominated by a kind of scientific weltanschauung which prevents us from seeing the significance of this crucial fact. He once wrote: "The fatal thing about the scientific way of thinking, which the whole world employs nowadays, is that it wants to produce an explanation in answer to each anxiety."[25] This has blinded us to our limitations and led us both to an arrogant overestimation of our power and significance in the broader scheme of things and to a loss of confidence in the powers that bear down upon and sustain us.

It is important to note from the start that Wittgenstein maintained a keen interest in, and a deep respect for, what he considered the legitimate practice of science itself. He originally did experimental research in aeronautics in Manchester before going to Cambridge to work with Russell. David Pinsent recorded an incident when Wittgenstein told a fellow student at Cambridge "to read some good book on some exact science, and see what honest thought is."[26] In his later life he still seemed to admire the "exact sciences," and when he worked in a physiology research laboratory during the Second World War, he designed experiments and undertook his research responsibilities with such enthusiasm and skill that his supervisor said it was too bad he had not been a physiologist instead of a philosopher.[27] His reservations about science tend to arise either when people reflect on scientific practices and try to give them a metaphysical underpinning,[28] or when scientific methods and assumptions are taken superficially and applied to areas of life for which they are inappropriate.[29] In these cases, the methods and assumptions of science come to constitute a weltanschauung which obscures its own limitations and obliterates everything else of value, including our own humanity. Sometimes he expresses deeper doubts about the practice of science itself, and on one occasion he even suggests that perhaps "there is nothing good or desirable about scientific knowledge and that mankind, in seeking it, is falling into a trap" (CV, p. 56).

Although Wittgenstein generally shows respect for the "exact sciences," as long as they are engaged rigorously and do not overreach their proper bounds, he also emphasizes that from within a scientific weltanschauung it is not possible to understand what he is doing. He declares: "Whether the typical western scientist will understand or appreciate me is a matter of indifference to me, because, after all, he does not understand the spirit in which I write" (MS, 109, 206).[30] Wittgenstein's own writings are neither scientific nor written in a scientific spirit. In the *Philosophical Investigations* he writes:

It was true to say that our considerations could not be scientific ones. . . . And we may not advance any kind of theory. There must not be anything hypothetical in our considerations. We must do away with all *explanation,* and description alone must take its place. (PI, #109)

Wittgenstein's divergence from the scientific spirit is marked throughout his writings by his efforts to dwell on description and to eschew the search for underlying principles and laws. He felt that "the difficult thing here is not, to dig down to the ground; no, it is to recognize the ground that lies before us as the ground" (RFM, p. 333). In another remark he suggests, "Our mistake is to look for an explanation where we ought to look at what happens as a 'protophenomenon'" (PI, #654–#655). Presumably a protophenomenon is not something we seek to understand in terms of something else— such as an underlying theory, or a history of development—but something which is irreducible and must be apprehended directly on its own terms.

Wittgenstein illustrates this point by means of an analogy: "People who are constantly asking 'why' are like tourists who stand in front of a building reading Baedeker and are so busy reading the history of its construction, etc., that they are prevented from *seeing* the building" (CV, p. 40). The irony, of course, is that the understanding and appreciation of the building which the tourist seeks through explanation can only be achieved through recognizing the significance of what already lies open to view. Wittgenstein makes a similar point when discussing Sir James Frazer's theory that the Beltane festival originated in a ritual of human sacrifice:

> We might put it this way: Anyone who wanted to impress us with the story of the Beltane festival would not need to explain the hypothesis of its origin anyway; he would only have to lay before us the material (which leads him to this hypothesis) and say nothing more. Here one may be inclined to say: "Of course, because the listener or reader will draw the conclusion himself!" But must he draw the conclusion explicitly? i.e., draw it at all? And what sort of conclusion is it? That this or that is *probable?*[31]

In Wittgenstein's view, nothing important can be left to chance. The logician, like the religious believer, cannot afford to trade in probabilities. The meaning he seeks must be fundamental and beyond dispute, and it must somehow already be apparent in the ritual itself. Wittgenstein continues:

> In the same way, the fact that on certain days children burn a straw man could make us uneasy, even if no explanation were given. Strange that they should celebrate by burning a *man!* What I want to say is: the solution is not any more disquieting than the riddle. (RFGB, p. 18)

The sense of mystery, horror and awe expressed in the ritual is already more certain than any possible hypothesis about its origin, so such a hypothesis is superfluous and distracting. In each of these cases Wittgenstein wants to argue that it is misguided to try to justify or account for a present phenomenon in terms of something behind or before it that is no more clear or reliable than what shows in the phenomenon itself.

Wittgenstein makes the same kind of point with respect to our efforts to solve or explain philosophical problems. These problems do reflect something real and troubling about our language, but as soon as we try to produce a solution or explanation, he suggests, we lose touch with our language and go astray. The way to solve philosophical problems often retraces the way someone is taught the meaning of a concept, say the concept of a game, in the first place. One gives examples and expects them to be taken in a certain way. The temptation to suppose that when we give examples the learner will see the point behind them which we were unable to express (PI, #71), is similar to the temptation to say that when we describe the Beltane Festival the reader will draw the conclusion about its origin for himself. The hypothesis adds nothing which is not already better expressed in the material that gave rise to the hypothesis. The appropriate method is to describe the relevant parts of our language, or the ritual, in such a way that the relief, or understanding, we seek comes of itself. Perhaps the most complete remark on this theme is in *Zettel:*

> Here the temptation is overwhelming to say something further, when everything has already been described.—Whence this pressure? What analogy, what wrong interpretation produces it?
>
> Here we come up against a remarkable and characteristic phenomenon in philosophical investigation: the difficulty—I might say—is not that of finding the solution but rather that of recognizing as the solution something that looks as if it were only a preliminary to it. "We have already said everything.—Not anything that follows from this, no, *this* itself is the solution!"
>
> This is connected, I believe, with our wrongly expecting an explanation, whereas the solution of the difficulty is a description, if we give it the right place in our considerations. If we dwell upon it, and do not try to get beyond it.
>
> The difficulty here is: to stop. (Z, #313–#314)[32]

Further efforts to explain or justify these descriptions are vain and can only lead us to things which are less clear and secure than what we are trying to establish. According to Wittgenstein, relief from philosophical problems comes once we appreciate and respect the ultimacy of certain grammatical facts, or "protophenomena," which tend to escape our notice because they are always before our eyes.

The notion of giving descriptions instead of seeking explanations is reflected in Wittgenstein's primary purpose for keeping a journal. Brian McGuinness mentions a number of peripheral motives—such as Wittgenstein's desire to imitate Keller's diaries and his need for a substitute for someone in whom he could confide,—but stresses that "its fundamental purpose, as far as he could see it, was to reach a true understanding of, to come to terms with, his life as it actually was: to settle accounts with himself."[33] Explanations tend to obscure our relation to what there is, and descriptions are meant to be a means to clarify this relation. By keeping a notebook of his thoughts and feelings on personal and spiritual matters, Wittgenstein hopes to bring these thoughts and feelings in line with how things really are, and when this is achieved there should be no discrepancy between what he writes and how he lives.

In the "Postscript" to *Recollections of Wittgenstein,* Rush Rhees includes a lengthy quote from Wittgenstein's unpublished manuscripts in order to illuminate a series of confessions Wittgenstein made in the 1930s to family and friends,[34] and this passage sheds important light on his purpose for keeping a notebook. Wittgenstein writes:

In my autobiography I must try both to recount my life truly and to *understand* it. For example, my unheroic *nature* must not show as an unfortunate irregularity but as an essential quality (not a virtue). If I may explain in a simile: If a street loafer were to write his biography, the danger would be that he would either

> (a) deny that his nature was what it is, or
> (b) would find some reason to be proud of it, or
> (c) present the matter as though this—that he has such a nature—were of no consequence.

In the first case he lies, in the second he mimics a trait of the natural aristocrat, that pride which is a *vitium splendidum* and which he cannot really have any more than a crippled body can have natural grace. In the third case he makes as it were the gesture of social democracy, placing culture above the rough bodily qualities—but this is a deception as well. He is what he is, and this is important and means something but is no reason for pride; on the other hand it is always the object of his self-respect. (MS, 110)

The autobiographer's path to self-respect is a narrow one—one must avoid the temptations to deny, to justify, or to depreciate the unseemliness of one's nature. This closely parallels the path to worldly asceticism described by Weber. A religious disenchantment with the world which recognizes the world as both real and evil—not illusory—is in effect steering a course between the temptations to deny, to justify, or to depreciate the evilness of the world. On the level of autobiography as well as on the level of our view of the world, explanations tend either to obscure our relation to what there is, or to obscure the significance of this relation. The process of giving descriptions, like adopting a vocation, should help us resist these dangers.

On the positive side, the way to avoid temptation and preserve self-respect is also the way to achieve originality. Wittgenstein writes:

Someone who does not lie is already original enough. Because, after all, any originality worth wishing for could not be a sort of clever trick, or a personal peculiarity, be it as distinctive as you like.

In fact the beginnings of good originality are already there if you do not want to be something you are not. And all this has been said before *much* better by other people. (CV, p. 60)

"Good" originality could not consist in hastily constructed fabrications, or artificial and idiosyncratic fantasies, but in something arising from the ground of our being, something from the richness and subtlety of what there is, that thereby produces in others an irresistible sense of recognition and appreciation.

The significance of the need to root originality and self-respect in how things are goes beyond Wittgenstein's purpose in writing personal journals to encompass the purpose of his philosophical writings as well. In *Culture and Value,* he writes:

> I might say: if the place I want to get to could only be reached by way of a ladder, I would give up trying to get there. For the place I really have to get to is a place I must already be at now.
> Anything that I might reach by climbing a ladder does not interest me. (CV, p. 7)

This was written in 1930 and clearly expresses Wittgenstein's commitment to what is ready to hand. However, this statement also seems to directly contradict the famous analogy at the end of the *Tractatus,* where he says that the propositions in his own book should eventually be recognized as nonsense and that they should be compared to a ladder that has to be thrown away once one has climbed up it (TLP, 6.54). But upon closer inspection this contrast to the end of the *Tractatus* is superficial and misleading, and it does not mean that Wittgenstein simply reversed his earlier way of thinking. The two references to ladders refer to two distinct issues. The one ladder represents the need for a will that is transformed and rid of its vain worldly ambitions. The other ladder represents the rejection of any contrivance which denies the full significance and reality of the world.[35] Both kinds of ladders appear throughout Wittgenstein's writings, and they represent a tension he is careful to maintain.

Returning for a moment to Wittgenstein's purpose for keeping a personal journal, we find a comparable tension between his desire to accept who he is and his desire to change himself. Rush Rhees suggests:

> We can see that if he gave himself the precept: "Don't want or try to be what you are not!" and also: "Try to become a different man!," there need be no conflict between these. "Try to become a different man!" would often be: "Try not to deceive yourself about what you are!"[36]

The point is not simply to be realistic, or to live by a pragmatic principle like, "Honesty is the best policy." The point is to maintain a peculiar kind of tension by being "in the world" but not "of the world"—a tension aptly described as "worldly asceticism." For Wittgenstein the stakes are spiritual in nature, and when pride and self-deception separate us from ultimate sustaining powers we are put, as it were, in immediate and absolute peril.

This is clearly a danger for philosophers as well as for autobiographers. In *Culture and Value* Wittgenstein advises, "Don't concern yourself with what, presumably, no one but you grasps!" and later, "God grant the philosopher insight into what lies in front of everyone's eyes" (CV, p. 63). In other words, the insight of the philosopher cannot be, as it were, a clever trick, but like the self-respect of the autobiographer, or the originality of the writer, it must consist in a special kind of recognition of what everyone already knows.

This returns us to the critique of explanation given in *Remarks on Frazer's Golden Bough,* where Wittgenstein speaks of how the meaning of a ritual must already be there before us. The awe of the Beltane Festival, for example, cannot depend on tracing it back to something hidden in the past, as if it took an anthropologist to show us the meaning being expressed in the ritual. Wittgenstein concludes:

> I think one reason why the attempt to find an explanation is wrong is that we have only to put together in the right way what we *know,* without adding anything, and the satisfaction we are trying to get from the explanation comes of itself.
>
> And here the explanation is not what satisfies us anyway. When Frazer begins by telling the story of the King of the Wood at Nemi, he does this in a tone which shows that something strange and terrible is happening here. And that is the answer to the question "why is this happening?": because it is terrible. In other words, what strikes us in this course of events as terrible, impressive, horrible, tragic, &c., anything but trivial and insignificant, *that* is what gave birth to them.
>
> We can only *describe* and say, human life is like that.
>
> Compared with the impression that what is described here makes on us, the explanation is too uncertain. (RFGB, pp. 2–3)

Here again we have Wittgenstein's point that our considerations cannot be hypothetical ones. The descriptions of rituals Wittgenstein is seeking, like his descriptions of logical grammar, should have an immediacy and self-evidence that makes them beyond dispute.

Though this way of seeing things is in direct contrast to the scientific spirit, it can easily be compared to a religious spirit. In a passage where Pears spells out the contrast between religion and science, he draws a distinction that bears a strong resemblance to the contrast Wittgenstein gives between logic and science. Pears writes: "Religious beliefs, unlike scientific beliefs, are not hypotheses, are not based on evidence, and cannot be regarded as more or less probable."[37] The logician, like the religious believer, should recognize that he is concerned with precisely those things which go without saying, which are not tentative or subject to empirical contingencies or chance, and hence that it is vain and futile to try to produce an explanation in answer to every question or anxiety. At some point our explanations will come to an end, so if understanding is ever to be achieved, or if anxiety is ever to be put to rest, it will not be on account of explanations and reassurances but on account of an attitude and a way of living that recognizes and embraces the ultimacy of the dictates of grammar from the start.

Our compulsion to seek explanations, Wittgenstein suggests, reveals a deep-rooted anxiety. This anxiety indicates a failure to live in the present, a failure to accept our dependence on that which bears down upon and sustains us. In *Culture and Value* Wittgenstein discusses these issues explicitly:

> The use of the word "fate." Our attitude to the future and the past. To what extent do we hold ourselves responsible for the future? How much do we speculate about the future? How do we think about the past and the future? If something unwelcome happens:—do we ask "Whose fault is it?," do we say "It must be somebody's fault,"— or do we say "It was God's will," "It was fate"?
>
> In the sense in which asking a question and insisting on an answer is expressive of a different attitude, a different mode of life, from not asking it, the *same* can be said of utterances like "It is God's will" or "We are not masters of our fate." The work done by this sentence, or at any rate something like it, could also be done by a command! Including one which you give yourself. And conversely the utterance of a command, such as "Don't be resentful," may be like the affirmation of a truth. (CV, p. 61)

Although this discussion is pitched on the level of specific ethical and religious forms of speech, two of the issues being raised are directly applicable to Wittgenstein's writings as a whole.

First, there is the issue of the similarity between certain kinds of assertions and commands. Wittgenstein frequently argues that utterances which are fundamental to one's way of seeing and being in the world may sometimes appear in the form of assertions about facts, but their unique normative role can be revealed by restating them as commands.[38] In the *Remarks on the Foundations of Mathematics,* Wittgenstein makes this point when he suggests that mathematical propositions could be expressed as commands. For example, the statement "$10 \times 10 = 100$" could be expressed in the imperative form, "Let $10 \times 10 = 100$" (RFM, p. 276)—though in this case there seems little reason to choose between them. But when the proposition has to do with predictions of matters of fact—for example, that a certain set of numbers will never occur in an infinite series, or more specifically, that "7777" will never occur in the extension of pi—then Wittgenstein finds the imperative form actually preferable to the statement of fact:

> Everyone feels uncomfortable at the thought that a proposition can state that such-and-such does not occur in an infinite series—while on the other hand there is nothing startling about a command's saying that this must not occur in this series however far it is continued.

But what is the source of this distinction between: "however far you go you will never find this"—and "however far you go you must never do this?"

The statement seems to overreach itself, the command not at all. (RFM, p. 276)

In this sense commands are similar to giving examples: "One gives examples and intends them to be taken in a particular way.—I do not, however, mean by this that he is supposed to see in those examples that common thing which I—for some reason—was unable to express; but that he is now to *employ* those examples in a particular way. Here giving examples is not an *indirect* means of explaining—in default of a better" (PI, #71). When Wittgenstein speaks of putting mathematical propositions in an imperative form, or giving examples, the point is that the foundation of our language, as well as our mathematics, consists in activities and skills, and one should obey commands as one should employ examples. On a fundamental level, understanding is not expressed in terms of facts, essences, or eternal truths, but in an ability to *do* things. Wittgenstein's desire to restrict mathematical propositions to what can be put in the form of commands seems to be closely related to his tendency to compare the dictates of logic to those of "the fearful judge." I have argued that the way Wittgenstein chose to speak about ethics—"Good is what God orders"—is an apt way to understand the nature of rule following in general. This brings us to the second issue.

Utterances like "It is God's will," or "We are not masters of our fate," are expressions of the general Wittgensteinian theme that there are powers which bear down upon and sustain us, that logical grammar is thrust upon us, and that we need to accept these conditions before we can do or say anything at all. In chapter 3 it was noted that he even views mathematical operations as dependent at each step on our previous submission to a kind of training, and still Wittgenstein would suggest, "A good angel is always necessary" (RFM, p. 378). However, in order to demonstrate the presence of a religious dimension in Wittgenstein's work, it is not enough to argue that Wittgenstein puts the bastion of logical and mathematical necessities afloat on a sea of contingencies. D. Z. Phillips is careful to point out that, "As far as a feeling of contingency is concerned, the feeling that we could be crushed at any moment, destroyed as persons, by external circumstances, that in itself is not a religious feeling. Religion enters when there is a certain response to that feeling."[39]

What kind of response to our absolute dependence on what is thrust upon us, would qualify as a religious response? Wittgenstein struggles to steer a course between denial and defiance on one hand and despair and resigned acceptance on the other. We have roughly described his response to the sense of dependency and contingency before arbitrary power—to the givenness of evil and grace—in terms of worldly asceticism, and a number of further aspects of Wittgenstein's attitude can be illuminated by this comparison. In the case of the Reformed tradition, where the Calvinist sense of contingency is particularly strong, James Gustafson suggests, "That Other evokes piety; a sense of awe and reverence, the senses of dependence, gratitude, obligation, repentance, possibilities for action, and direction."[40]

As a description of a religious response to the forces which bear down upon and sustain us, these attitudes are not unique to Protestant Christianity but are important features of rituals in general. Indeed, this is why Wittgenstein's discussion of rituals in *Remarks on Frazer's "Golden Bough"* can be used to criticize our tendency to demand explanations. We pursue explanations as if the meaning of our actions depended primarily on their causes and consequences. An examination of rituals shows how misguided and hopeless this pursuit can be. The point of a ritual is to express a sense of participation in fundamental realities, or to express certain attitudes toward them—a sense of awe and respect perhaps—and not to express knowledge claims about these realities. Wittgenstein writes: "What makes the character of ritual action is not any view or opinion, either right or wrong, although an opinion—a belief—itself can be ritualistic, or belong to a rite" (RFGB, p. 7). The meaning of a ritual does not rest on a set of assertions about underlying facts but on the activity itself, and so a meaningful performance of the ritual need not entail a "belief" in, or "knowledge" of, the various prerequisite facts. In this, Wittgenstein suggests, it resembles other activities which are crucial to a form of life: "Does a child believe that milk exists? Or does it know that milk exists? Does a cat know that a mouse exists?" (OC, #478). Fundamental activities like drinking milk and catching mice are prior to any explicit knowledge or opinion about what is the case. They depend on certain skills in which we engage unreflectively as part of a way of life, and all we can say is that if milk and mice did not exist, then the practices of drinking milk and catching mice would cease to exist as well. These practices, like rituals, can be viewed as "protophenomena" that characterize particular forms of life.

Wittgenstein's tendency to view knowledge in terms of an ability to do things, and to replace questions about the meaning of words with questions about their use, naturally leads to comparisons with pragmatism.[41] Wittgenstein saw this as a danger and he explicitly warns against making this analogy: "So I am trying to say something that sounds like pragmatism. Here I am being thwarted by a kind of *Weltanschauung*" (OC, 422). Wittgenstein characterizes the weltanschauung of our modern industrial civilization in terms of its commitment to ever larger forms and endless progress. If we take Wittgenstein's emphasis on "use" in light of the spirit of our age, it appears to imply that the meaning of a word is reducible to its practical consequences. This conclusion is encouraged by Wittgenstein's tendency to compare words with practical instruments—like tools or the handles in a locomotive (PI, #11–#12)—a comparison which confuses the point that words can only be understood as part of an activity, with the idea that words can only be understood in light of their utility. The latter idea reduces "use" to what is "useful," where words and practices are seen solely in terms of their efficacy in bringing about our goals.

For the most part, Wittgenstein is not being pragmatic in this sense. The meaning of numbers, for example, should be understood by how they are used in counting, doing sums, etc., but he does not think this implies that "use" can be reduced to utility. He asks rhetorically: "Why do we count? Has it proved practical? Do we have the concepts we have, e.g. our psychological concepts, because it has proved advantageous?—And yet we do have *certain* concepts on that account, we have introduced them on that account" (Z, #700). Wittgenstein does not deny that some practices arise from considerations of utility. He just doubts that such practices are typical.

In Wittgenstein's view, "use" frequently articulates, preserves and celebrates meaning, more like a religious ritual than as an instrument to an end. In response to Frazer's tendency to treat magical practices as a pseudoscience, he writes: "Burning in effigy. Kissing the picture of a loved one. This is obviously *not* based on a belief that it will have a definite effect on the object which the picture represents. It aims at some satisfaction and it achieves it. Or rather, it does not *aim* at anything; we act in this way and then feel satisfied" (RFGB, p. 4). If there are considerations of utility at work here they are secondary and inessential. The immediate meaning of these actions is more certain and fundamental than any accompanying thoughts about possible future events. On another occasion Wittgenstein writes:

> The characteristic feature of primitive man, I believe, is that he does not act from *opinions* he holds about things (as Frazer thinks).
> I read, amongst many similar examples, of a rain-king in Africa to whom the people appeal for rain *when the rainy season comes*. But surely this means that they do not actually think he can make rain, otherwise they would do it in the dry periods in which the land is "a parched and arid desert." For if we do assume that it was stupidity that once led the people to institute this office of Rain King, still they obviously knew from experience that the rains begin in March, and it would have been the Rain King's duty to perform in other periods of the year. Or again: towards morning, when the sun is

about to rise, people celebrate rites of the coming of day, but not at night, for then they simply burn lamps. (RFGB, p. 12)

Rituals, according to Wittgenstein, should not be viewed as some kind of pseudoscience involving primitive efforts to relate causes and effects. In response to another example of a practice that Frazer says is based on naivete and delusion, Wittgenstein declares: "If the adoption of a child is carried out by the mother pulling the child from beneath her clothes, then it is crazy to think there is an *error* in this and that she believes she has borne the child" (RFGB, p. 4).[42] This rite of adoption is not intended as an objective description of a fact, any more than consulting the Rain King and celebrating rites of the coming of day are primitive attempts at the sciences of meteorology and physics, flawed attempts to understand and intervene in the physical world. The purpose of these practices is entirely different. Rituals express a sense of participation in the larger cosmos, and a sense of awe, respect and gratitude before the fundamental sustaining powers.

In a similar way, Wittgenstein believes that practices in general are ritualistic in character even today and are not simply motivated by their utility. Again, he asks rhetorically: "Does man think, then, because he has found that thinking pays?—Because he thinks it is advantageous to think? (Does he bring his children up because he has found it pays?)" (PI, #467). Wittgenstein is suggesting that most of what we do in our lives is prior to any consideration of its possible consequences. We are sustained by a network of ritual practices which are followed as a matter of course.[43]

Under the influence of our modern weltanschauung, we tend to deny our place in the broader scheme of things, or we try to defy it, but the first condition of seeing things from a religious point of view is to recognize our profound dependence on things and forces which are beyond our control. The second condition is to embrace these realities in a special spirit, without a sense of fatalism and resignation. James Edwards describes such a generic religious attitude as follows:

From this "religious" perspective, the fundamental, normative relationship between the person and reality is, in its most general description, *harmony.* The person naturally desires to live in harmony with the realities which create and support him; true harmony with them is the basic aim of human life; and its achievement is human virtue. The specification of what counts as such harmony varied from culture to culture, of course; but in almost all cases, from Hebrew to Greek, the harmony was thought to be gained by some kind of immediate personal (including community) encounter with the realities. This personal relationship was facilitated and evidenced by certain forms of life adopted by the culture, forms of life designed to propitiate, to honor, to worship, to attend to, the various realities underlying human life. The realities to be encountered, and thus acknowledged, are the natural element within which the person lives and dies. Person and element are made for one another; there is no necessary distance, no barrier to be bridged. To live in harmony is to dwell in the world as the trout in the stream, supported by the elements of one's life as the water supports the fish, bringing air and nourishment as a matter of course. Or not. It is to dwell within, not without.

A crucial point to be noted is the immediacy of that relationship. In the "religious" attitude, the realities with which persons must live in harmony are apprehended *concretely and immediately.*[44]

This is a powerful and, for the most part, apt picture of what it would mean to dwell "within" a form of life, and it shows the inappropriateness of comparing such a way of life to a kind of utilitarianism.

However, the problem with this picture is that it is an overly romantic and idealized description that does not do justice to the seriousness of sin, a concern which we have found to be omnipresent in Wittgenstein's own writings. Edwards paints a picture, as it were, of life in the garden of Eden before the Fall. Wittgenstein expresses a strong sense that this natural order is corrupted, that the world is fraught with temptations, and that our willful desires constantly lead us astray from the way shown by logical grammar. Our fallen state is nowhere more clearly evident than in the perpetual nature of our philosophical confusions. Wittgenstein declares, "A philosophical problem has the form: 'I don't know my way about'" (PI #123), and elsewhere he observes, "If a man feels lost, that is the ultimate torment" (CV p. 46e). It is in light of a similar experience of aimlessness and despair that St. Augustine writes in the beginning of his *Confessions,* "Our hearts are restless until they can find peace in You."[45] Wittgenstein is looking for an end to philosophical torments, for a resting place, for thoughts that are at peace. Edwards offers a description of what it would mean to be no longer restless, to know one's way about in an immediate and concrete way—like fish in the sea. Wittgenstein, like Augustine before him, never achieves this rest for himself. He remains troubled by the effects of our alienation, by the discrepancy between this religious vision and our own restless lives.

Given our fallen condition, Wittgenstein sees rituals as limited efforts to harmonize with ultimate realities. Within a ritual the faithful act out their participation in these realities, and insofar as the performance is in good faith, they come to know their way about, as Edwards says, "immediately and concretely." At the same time, their submission to the forms of the ritual demonstrates their piety. It expresses a respect and awe of that which is immeasurably greater than themselves. Wittgenstein writes:

How could fire or fire's resemblance to the sun have failed to make an impression on the awakening mind of man? But not "because he can't explain it" (the stupid superstition of our time)—for does an "explanation" make it less impressive? . . .

I do not mean that it is especially *fire* that must make an impression on anyone. Fire no more than any other phenomenon, and one will impress this person and another that. For no phenomenon is particularly mysterious in itself, but any of them can become so to us, and it is precisely the characteristic feature of the awakening human spirit that a phenomenon has meaning for it. We could almost say, man is a ceremonious animal. This is partly false, partly nonsensical, but there is also something in it. (RFGB, pp. 6–7)

Any phenomenon can become ritualized into a "protophenomenon," an irreducible event which not only represents a focal point in our lives—an event in relation to which other events are understood—but also an event which comes to represent the mystery of what is greater than ourselves and both bears down upon and supports us. Wittgenstein sees this not as an embarrassing residue of a primitive stage of human development, but as a "characteristic feature of the awakening human spirit," a feature which has to do with ascribing significance to something and which remains a condition for the possibility of meaning even today. In *On Certainty* he declares that "any logic good enough for a primitive means of communication needs no apology from us. Language did not emerge from some kind of ratiocination" (OC, 475). In this sense his hesitant remark that "man is a ceremonious animal," is as crucial to understanding his philosophy as the remark, "Man is a rational animal," is crucial to understanding Aristotle's.

Wittgenstein believes that the basic way a ritual can effect piety is more general than Frazer thinks. Wittgenstein even goes so far as to suggest that the various possibilities for expressing piety can easily be imagined today because the fundamental principle of how a ritual effects piety is still with us. In one way or another it has to eschew the mundane, stepping apart from the probable contingencies of life to represent something of fundamental significance, a necessity grounded in nothing but mystery. He gives these examples:

We can readily imagine that, say, in a given tribe no-one is allowed to see the king, or again that every man in the tribe is obliged to see him. And then it will certainly not be left more or less to chance, but the king will be *shown* to the people. Perhaps no one will be allowed to touch him, or perhaps they will be *compelled* to do so. Think how after Schubert's death his brother cut certain of Schubert's scores into small pieces and gave to his favourite pupils these pieces of a few bars each. As a sign of piety this action is *just* as comprehensible to us as the other one of keeping the scores undisturbed and accessible to no-one. And if Schubert's brother had burnt the scores we could still understand this as a sign of piety.

The ceremonial (hot or cold) as opposed to the haphazard (lukewarm) is a characteristic of piety. (RFGB, p. 5)

This resonates with the words of Revelation: "I know thy works, that thou art neither cold nor hot: I would thou wert cold or hot. So then because thou art lukewarm, and neither cold nor hot, I shall spit you out of my mouth."[46] The piety of Wittgenstein's writings on logic and grammar can be compared to the ritual piety expressed before the king. The apprehension of logical form, like seeing the king, "will certainly not be left more or less to chance, but [it] will be *shown* to the people." For Wittgenstein, mundane matters of fact may or may not be the case and propositions about them can be "said" in a common everyday sort of way, but logic itself must not be profaned in this pedestrian manner. It can only be "shown" in a way that sets it apart from the mundane world and preserves a kind of ritual purity. Necessity rests, as it were, on the mystery of ritual piety.

We have quoted Gustafson's claim that an awareness of the contingency of our lives, institutions and aspirations lies at the root of religiosity: "the Other evokes piety; a sense of awe and reverence, the senses of dependence, gratitude, obligation, repentance, possibilities for action, and direction."[47] Historically, before Protestant Christianity challenged the role of the Church and the priesthood as mediators between God and humanity, these religious attitudes were expressed largely through periodic sacred religious rites which took place in special places at special times set apart from the profane routines of our worldly existence. To compare Wittgenstein's attitude to worldly asceticism is to suggest that for him this distinction has collapsed and that all of the aspects of our worldly existence—the daily routines of work, politics, family life, and leisure—have become a means of ritualized religious expression.[48] Without something like ritual piety, there would be no logical form at all. In other words, meaning itself is fundamentally ritualistic—it rests on a mysterious agreement in judgments, in forms of life—and the whole of our worldly activities, the whole of logical grammar, should express an appropriate sense of piety, awe, reverence and gratitude. I want to suggest that it is considerations such as these which are behind Wittgenstein's expressed desire to say that the *Philosophical Remarks* is "written to the glory of God" (PR, Foreword, p. 7).

To illustrate what it might mean for Wittgenstein's philosophical work to be written to the glory of God, we can return to Wittgenstein's critique of explanation. With a high degree of misapprehension Robert Fogelin characterizes the enduring impulse behind Wittgenstein's treatment of explanation in a way that shows its religious nature, but he fails to recognize its significance in these terms. In his summary Fogelin quotes a remark from the *Philosophical Investigations:*

Don't take it as a matter of course, but as a remarkable fact, that pictures and fictitious narratives give us pleasure, occupy our minds.

("Don't take it as matter of course" means: find it surprising, as you do some things which disturb you. *Then the puzzling aspect of the latter will disappear, by your accepting this fact as you do the other.*) (PI, #524 [Fogelin's italics])

Fogelin interprets this remark as follows:

If we take this parenthetical remark seriously—and I have no doubt that it is intended seriously—we get a procedure that is just the reverse of explanation. In an explanation we often try to remove the strangeness of something by showing how it is derived from (or fits in with) things that are not strange. Wittgenstein suggests that instead we should be struck with the strangeness of the familiar and in this way the original case will lose its exceptional character. Thus instead of eliminating the contrast between the strange and the obvious by making everything obvious, Wittgenstein would have us eliminate this contrast by recognizing that everything is strange.[49]

In other words, Wittgenstein tries to release us from our obsession with philosophical problems, not by solving the problems or by reducing them to more palatable terms, but by showing that all the things we take for granted are just as puzzling and mysterious as the things which bother us, and hence that it is vain and misguided to try to solve the original problems. Fogelin seems to find this recurrent strand in Wittgenstein untenable, even absurd. I believe Fogelin's description of what Wittgenstein is doing is fair and perceptive—he just fails to see the point in the proper light. We are now in a position to suggest that what Fogelin describes as "the reverse of explanation" is part of what Wittgenstein meant when he spoke of "seeing every problem from a religious point of view."[50]

Thematically, Wittgenstein tries to show us the marvels which lie right before our eyes. In the *Philosophical Investigations* he takes everyday activities like giving ostensive definitions and teaching the application of mathematical formulas, and argues that these definitions and formulas themselves do not determine a unique application. In this light there is something amazing about the everyday fact that the interlocutor, or student, generally catches the "right" meaning from among an assortment of possible interpretations and goes on to do as we expect. We should recognize that there is something surprising and deeply significant even in our most common activities.

In the context of music Wittgenstein's tendency to see something extraordinary in what appears ordinary takes a slightly different form:

The last two bars of the "Death and the Maiden" theme. . . ; it's possible to understand this at first as an ordinary, conventional figure before coming to understand its deeper expression. I.e. before coming to understand that what is ordinary is here filled with significance. (CV, p. 52)

In a passage from *Remarks on Frazer's "Golden Bough,"* where Wittgenstein is discussing myths and what it means to have a point of view, he reflects on these transformations more directly: "We might say 'every view has its charm,' but this would be wrong. What is true is that every view is significant for him who sees it so (but that does not mean 'sees it as something other than it is'). And in this sense every view is equally significant" (RFGB, p. 11). I have argued that in the Protestant ethic all kinds of work can have religious value in the eyes of God as long as the work is engaged as a calling, a worldly occupation which is dedicated to the glory of God,[51] and in this sense all occupations have equal significance. The way value can be attributed to a point of view is similar to the way Divine sanction is attributed to work in the Protestant ethic. In either case, what appears ordinary and routine can take on an ultimate value and significance.

Once, after recounting Engelmann's experience of finding his entire collection of manuscripts splendid, only to have them lose their charm and value as soon as he considered making a selection of them available for publication, Wittgenstein reflects on the difference between a mundane and a Divine perspective:

Nothing could be more remarkable than seeing a man who thinks he is unobserved performing some quite simple everyday activity. Let us imagine a theatre; the curtain goes up and we see a man alone in a room, walking up and down, lighting a cigarette, sitting down, etc. so that suddenly we are observing a human being from outside in a way that ordinarily we can never observe ourselves; . . . We should be observing something more wonderful than anything a playwright could arrange to be acted or spoken on the stage: life itself.—But then we do see this every day without its making the slightest impression on us! True enough, but we do not see it from *that* point of view.—Well, when E. looks at what he has written and finds it marvelous (even though he would not care to publish any of the pieces individually), he is seeing his life as a work of art created by God and, as such, it is certainly worth contemplating, as is every life and everything whatever. (CV, p. 4)

To speak of something as created by God is to view it from outside the preestablished horizon which is the precondition for language. This passage is fully consistent with Wittgenstein's remarks in the *Notebooks* that ethics is the world viewed *sub specie aeternitatis* and that aesthetics is an object viewed *sub specie aeternitatis* (NB, p. 83e). In this view, value cannot be determined from amidst the world, from amidst logical form, and consequently questions of value are inexpressible in language. However, in speaking of seeing things as created by God, Wittgenstein is clearly suggesting that language does not exhaust human experience and that we can in some way be receptive to matters of value.

The importance of seeing one's life and world as God's handiwork is an important theme throughout the Judeo-Christian tradition. In his *Confessions,* for example, St. Augustine recounts a twofold story of his life in order to address the problem of the will. On the one hand he recounts a narrative of sin, where every thought and event in his life is viewed in terms of his sinful earthly concerns. On the other hand he recounts a narrative of grace, where the same thoughts and events were used by God to bring about his eventual salvation. In this sense Augustine endeavors to see his life as a work of art created by God, and in so doing he hopes to release the hold that the mundane way of thinking and feeling has on his life.

When, instead of reducing puzzles and peculiarities to things that appear common and plausible, Wittgenstein shows us the strangeness of the familiar, he is trying to shift our perspective from the mundane to the religious and to recapture the special sense of wonder and awe which he felt was extinguished by the prevailing scientific weltanschauung. A more direct, and less apologetic, way to describe what Fogelin calls "the reverse of explanation," is to say that Wittgenstein strives to look at everything as though it were a miracle.

Wittgenstein alludes to the idea of miracles periodically throughout his writings,[52] but the most clear and developed treatment occurs in his discussion of the difference between relative and absolute values in the "Lecture on Ethics." He writes:

We all know what in ordinary life would be called a miracle. It obviously is simply an event the like of which we have never yet seen. Now suppose such an event happened. Take the case that one of you suddenly grew a lion's head and began to roar. Certainly that would be as extraordinary a thing as I can imagine. Now whenever we should have recovered from our surprise, what I would suggest would be to fetch a doctor and have the case scientifically investigated and if it were not for hurting him I would have him vivisected. And where would the miracle have got to? For it is clear that when we look at it in this way everything miraculous has disappeared; unless what we mean by this term is merely that a fact has not yet been explained by science which again means that we have hitherto failed to group this fact with others in a scientific system. This shows that it is absurd to say "Science has proved that there are no miracles." The truth is that the scientific way of looking at a fact is not the way to look at it as a miracle. (LE, pp. 10–11)

Wittgenstein is suggesting, to begin with, that seeing something as a miracle involves taking it as a protophenomenon, a thing or event which is not placed within a scientific system but is considered unique and irreducible. Furthermore, he suggests that a miracle must be received in a particular spirit—it must be seen as a testimony to the mystery and majesty of ultimate powers. Wittgenstein offers this example:

The miracles of nature.
   One might say: art *shows* us the miracles of nature. It is based on the *concept* of the miracles of nature. (The blossom, just opening out. What is *marvelous* about it?) We say: "Just look at it opening out!" (CV, p. 56)

The intrinsic value which is often attributed to works of art and works of nature alike is made possible, Wittgenstein suggests, by treating such things as miracles rather than as objects for scientific investigation.

   On the one hand, Wittgenstein wants to say that a phenomenon, any phenomenon, can be viewed as a miracle, as "an event the like of which we have never yet seen." On the other hand, he wants to say that a miracle can be treated like an event or a fact just like any other, and hence that it is always susceptible to scientific investigation. When things are seen in this way there may be riddles, but there is no room for anything miraculous.[53] Wittgenstein continues:

The mathematician too can wonder at the miracles (the crystal) of nature of course; but can he do so once a problem has arisen about *what* it actually is he is contemplating? Is it really possible as long as the object that he finds astonishing and gazes at with awe is *shrouded* in a philosophical fog?
   I could imagine somebody might admire not only real trees, but also the shadows or reflections that they cast, taking them too for trees. But once he has told himself that these are not really trees after all and has come to be puzzled at what they are, or at how they are related to trees, his admiration will have suffered a rupture that will need healing. (CV, p. 57)

Wittgenstein makes a similar point in a remark written seventeen years earlier: "Man has to awaken to wonder—and so perhaps do peoples. Science is a way of sending him to sleep again" (CV, p. 5). Once an object of wonder and awe has become a riddle to be solved, an object to be placed within a scientific system, our respect for its immediate and intrinsic value is lost.

   Wittgenstein's sense that all things and activities are as unique and irreducible as miracles bears close affinities to occasionalism,[54] not only in terms of the philosophical doctrine, but also in terms of the religious sensitivities it frequently expresses. Occasionalism has often been embraced by thinkers who were particularly concerned to emphasize the limitations of human reason and the omnipotence and glory of God. Consider the point that in the *Tractatus* Wittgenstein leaves no room in the world for laws like inertia or causality. Each moment is absolutely independent of the others, and the facts found in one instance do not justify our expectations about what facts will follow in the next instance. If things appear to follow scientific laws over time it is only owing, as it were, to the grace of God. Likewise in the *Investigations,* Wittgenstein argues that there is nothing in a mathematical formula or a grammatical rule which determines the continuity of application or meaning from one instance to the next, and again, "A good angel is always necessary" (RFM, p. 378)—it is only owing to something akin to the grace of God that formulas and rules have the usefulness that they do.

In a passage clearly inspired by Wittgenstein, and also resembling certain occasionalist ideas found in the writings of someone like Malebranche, Rush Rhees writes:

> Anyway, I cannot see that the idea of a *beginning* of things is so important for religion. Or rather, I cannot see *why* it is. The belief that God is the *source* of the world, and that everything in the world has its reality from God—I can see that that is important. But just for that reason, I wonder whether the beginning depended on God in any other sense than the present does.

For the occasionalists, the extent of our dependence on God is expressed by the doctrine that God actively maintains the being of the world; He recreates the world in its entirety from moment to moment, so "the beginning" was no more contingent and miraculous than the present is. Rhees continues:

> The question is much more ' *Why* is there anything at all? What is the sense of it?'
> Or it may be an expression of wonder at the world. ('Isn't it extraordinary that anything at all should exist?') Which easily passes into reverence at the wonder of it—the wonder at there being anything at all. There is gratitude in this too—gratitude for the existence of things.[55]

Our compulsion to explain not only presupposes the continuity of the nature and behavior of things—blinding us to the mysteries which lie at the root of our most common daily activities—but it leads us to take being itself for granted and to forget the ultimate question, "Why is there anything at all?"[56]

Throughout Wittgenstein's writings he advocates a change in our manner of *seeing.* The *Tractatus* ends with the claim that we must come to "see the world aright" (TLP, 6.54), and the *Philosophical Investigations* is full of allusions to our failure to see what is right before our eyes. This in turn requires not understanding but a change of will, and it is to this end that Wittgenstein often draws our attention to the marvels which go unnoticed because of their familiarity. Pride and conceit must give way to a sense of appreciation and wonder if we are to recognize and accept what bears down upon and sustains us, if our will is to be transformed in accordance to "the will of God."

In this way Wittgenstein establishes an intimate connection between the violation of language and a distinctly moral failing, a pretense and perversity of the will. The limits of language mark the limits of our world, and through reflection on logical form we ought to recognize the inherent duplicity of our failure to acknowledge ourselves and our world as they really are. The idea is to accept these things as they are without taking them for granted and to experience the everyday as though it were a testimony to "the glory of God." By framing our failure to abide within the limits of language in terms of "sin," Wittgenstein suggests the depth of our dependence on and obligation to logical form, but by the same analogy the ultimacy of logical form shows us something of what it would mean to speak of the sovereignty and glory of God.

NOTES

1. Logic and Sin

1. Wittgenstein emphasized this point in an undated letter to Ludwig von Ficker, probably written in early November 1919 ("Letters to Ludwig von Ficker," ed. Allan Janik, in *Wittgenstein: Sources and Perspectives,* ed. C. G. Luckhardt [Ithaca, N.Y.: Cornell University Press, 1979]).

2. Ludwig Wittgenstein, *Philosophical Remarks,* ed. G. H. von Wright and G. E. M. Anscombe, trans. G. E. M. Anscombe (Oxford: Basil Blackwell, 1953), p. 7; hereafter cited in text as PR.

3. This assertion appears four times on the first page of the notebook and again on page eleven (*Notebooks: 1914–1916,* 2d ed. [Chicago: University of Chicago Press, 1979], pp. 2, 11; hereafter cited in text as NB).

4. Wittgenstein, *Culture and Value,* ed. G. H. von Wright in collaboration with Heikki Nyman, trans. Peter Winch (Chicago: University of Chicago Press, 1980), p. 7e; hereafter cited in text as CV.

5. M. O'C. Drury, "Some Notes on Conversations With Wittgenstein," *Recollections of Wittgenstein,* ed. Rush Rhees (Oxford: Oxford University Press, 1984), p. 79.

6. The most interesting and prolific writer I have in mind is D. Z. Phillips (see, for example, his *Faith and Philosophical Enquiry* [London: Routledge & Kegan Paul, 1970]). Other writers might include Alan Keightley (*Wittgenstein, Grammar and God* [London: Epworth Press, 1976]); Dallas M. High (*Language, Persons, and Belief* [New York: Oxford University Press, 1967]); William Hordern (*Speaking of God* [New York: Macmillan, 1964]); W. Donald Hudson (*Wittgenstein and Religious Belief,* New Studies in the Philosophy of Religion [New York: St. Martin's Press, 1975]); John A. Hutchison (*Language and Faith* [Philadelphia: The Westminster Press, 1963]); Fredrick Ferré (*Language, Logic and God* [Chicago: University of Chicago Press, 1981]); and Ignace D'hert O. P. (*Wittgenstein's Relevance for Theology,* European University Papers, series 23: Theology, vol. 44 [Bern: Herbert Lang & Co. Ltd., 1974]).

7. Bertrand Russell, "Philosophers and Idiots," *The Listener* 55 (February 1955): 247.

8. Norman Malcolm, *Ludwig Wittgenstein: A Memoir,* with a biographical sketch by G. H. von Wright, 2d ed., with Wittgenstein's letters to Malcolm (Oxford: Oxford University Press, 1984), pp. 23–81.

9. Bartley suggests that Wittgenstein's efforts in the *Tractatus* to exclude ethics

from the domain of language is motivated by a desire to protect his homosexual tendencies from censure (*Wittgenstein,* 2d ed., revised and enlarged [LaSalle, Ill.: Open Court, 1985]).

10. Brian McGuinness, *Wittgenstein, a Life: Young Ludwig (1889–1921)* (Berkeley and Los Angeles: University of California Press, 1988). See, for example, page 53, though this theme is present throughout the biography.

11. Ray Monk, *Ludwig Wittgenstein: The Duty of Genius* (New York: The Free Press, 1990).

12. Otto Weininger was the author of *Sex and Character,* trans. anonymous (London: William Heinemann, 1906), a bizarre and disturbing book which drew broad sweeping distinctions between "Woman" as a purely sensual and soulless being, and the "genius" as the man who overcomes the sensual "Womanish" aspects of his nature in order to live a spiritual life according to reason and the knowledge of good and evil. Given this situation, Weininger concludes that in effect we are faced with a severe moral imperative: either achieve genius or choose death. Weininger himself became a sensational cult figure in Vienna when in 1903, at the age of 23, he acted upon his theory and committed suicide in the house where Beethoven died.

13. Monk, *The Duty of Genius,* p. 25.

14. Carl Pletsch, *Young Nietzsche: Becoming a Genius* (New York: The Free Press, 1991).

15. Monk, *The Duty of Genius,* p. 25.

16. This way of resolving the tension between the genius trope and the religious trope was suggested by an anonymous reader.

17. Pletsch, *Young Nietzsche,* pp. 1, 11.

18. The recent study by Cyril Barrett, *Wittgenstein, Ethics and Religious Belief* (Oxford: Basil Blackwell, 1991), seeks to address this same issue by working through Wittgenstein's explicit remarks on ethics and religious belief.

19. In the *Tractatus* Wittgenstein writes: "Language disguises thought. So much so, that from the outward form of the clothing it is impossible to infer the form of the thought beneath it, because the outward form of the clothing is not designed to reveal the form of the body, but for entirely different purposes" (*Tractatus Logico-Philosophicus,* trans. D. F. Pears and B. F. McGuinness, with an intro. by Bertrand Russell [London: Routledge and Kegan Paul, 1961], 4.002; hereafter cited in text as TLP). In a remark early in the *Philosophical Investigations* a similar idea is expressed: "Of course, what confuses us is the uniform appearance of words when we hear them spoken or meet them in script and print. For their *application* is not presented to us so clearly" (*Philosophical Investigations,* ed. G. H. von Wright and G. E. M. Anscombe, trans. G. E. M. Anscombe [Oxford: Basil Blackwell, 1953], remark #11; hereafter cited in text as PI); or again: "If we look at the example in #1, we may perhaps get an inkling how much this general notion of the meaning of a word surrounds the working of language with a haze which makes clear vision impossible. It disperses the fog to study the phenomena of language in primitive kinds of application in which one can command a clear view of the aim and functioning of the words" (PI, #5).

20. Anthony Kenny, "Wittgenstein on the Nature of Philosophy," *Wittgenstein and His Times,* ed. Brian McGuinness (Chicago: University of Chicago Press, 1982), p. 15.

21. William James, *The Varieties of Religious Experience: A Study in Human Nature,* being the Gifford Lectures on Natural Religion delivered at Edinburgh in 1901–1902, with a foreword by Jacques Barzun (New York: The New American Library, Inc., n.d.), p. 363.

22. Drury, "Conversations," in *Recollections,* ed. Rhees, 1984), p. 88.

23. For some examples see Norman Malcolm, *A Memoir,* pp. 23–31; Fania Pascal, "A Personal Memoir," *Recollections,* ed. Rhees, pp. 23, 29, 31–39; John King, "Recollections of Wittgenstein," ibid., pp. 70, 75; and in the collection of essays *Ludwig Wittgenstein: The Man and His Philosophy,* ed. K. T. Fann (New Jersey: Humanities Press, 1967), see G. H. von Wright, "A Biographical Sketch," pp. 26–27; Rudolf Carnap, p. 34; D. A. T. Gasking and A. C. Jackson, "Wittgenstein as Teacher," pp. 52, 54; Karl Britton, "Portrait of a Philosopher," pp. 57, 62; and Wolfe Mays, "Recollections of Wittgenstein," pp. 80, 82.

24. James, *Varieties,* p. 47. This characterization of Wittgenstein is in striking contrast to Richard Rorty's suggestion in "Keeping Philosophy Pure" (*Yale Review* 65 [Spring 1976]: 336–356) that Wittgenstein "just makes fun of" the traditional problems of philosophy (p. 354), as if Wittgenstein's writings could be read as a series of jokes. While Kierkegaard, "the world-historical jester," shows how serious jokes can be, what Rorty seems to mean by this, as shown by his frequently flippant use of ridicule and sharp wit to undermine metaphysical pretense, runs counter to what I perceive as the central thrust of Wittgenstein's life's work—its profound and serious commitment to that which makes meaning possible. In "Keeping Philosophy Pure" Rorty contrasts Wittgenstein to those who seek to replace an incorrect view of the problems of modern philosophy with a correct view. Rorty writes: "When Wittgenstein is at his best, he resolutely avoids such constructive criticism and sticks to pure satire" (p. 354). Again, satire is often terribly serious, having the intention of restoring a proper sense of priorities, but Rorty seems to take "pure satire" to be purely negative, as if Wittgenstein, "at his best," was simply clearing the decks. In light of James' description it is precisely Wittgenstein's seriousness, his deep commitment to that which makes meaning possible, that differentiates him from Rorty, and where Rorty attributes this seriousness to an uncharacteristic lapse into problematic and extraneous metaphysical concerns, I would hold it to be an integral part of Wittgenstein's work.

25. Malcolm, *A Memoir,* p. 28.

26. In recounting a meeting of the Moral Sciences Club long after their relationship had deteriorated, Wittgenstein once remarked that Russell was "most disagreeable. Glib and superficial, though, as always, *astonishingly* quick" (*Letters to Russell, Keynes and Moore,* ed. G. H. von Wright [Oxford: Blackwell, 1974], p. 186). Also see McGuinness, *A Life,* pp. 194–196.

27. In giving a "description" I am not only setting aside questions of historical influence, I am also setting aside psychological questions of the extent to which Wittgenstein was conscious of his use of religious themes.

28. This point is made obliquely in a letter to Russell dated 12 June 1919, and more directly in a letter on 19 August 1919 (*Letters to Russell, Keynes and Moore,* pp. 69–73).

29. While there is much written on Wittgenstein and religion there is virtually no discussion of sin in the literature—in spite of the fact that a sense of sin appears as the

most obvious and significant religious structure appearing in Wittgenstein's writings. Perhaps this is a function of the fact that, among those sensitive to religious themes, Wittgenstein has been largely adopted by those who seem to consider sin passé and who are more concerned with establishing a theoretical basis for religious pluralism and with carving out a niche where religious discourse can escape the empiricist critique. These philosophers and theologians tend to be blind to the ways Wittgenstein's writings follow in the path of thinkers William James calls "sick souls"—those like St. Augustine, Pascal, Calvin, Jonathan Edwards, and Kierkegaard.

2. The Limit

1. Both are translations of *eine Grenze.*

2. David Pears observes that the determinateness of sense is an axiom Wittgenstein takes over from Frege (*Ludwig Wittgenstein* [Cambridge: Harvard University Press, 1986], p. 76). While Wittgenstein wavered in the *Notebooks* on the question of whether things could be infinitely divisible (NB, p. 62), he eventually decided that there must be simples by linking it to the determinateness of sense: "The requirement that simple signs be possible is the requirement that sense be determinate" (TLP, 3.23).

3. Leszek Kolakowski, *Religion* (New York: Oxford University Press, 1982), p. 174.

4. There has been long-standing debates over how to interpret Wittgenstein's remarks on "showing." Given our limited purposes an extensive discussion of these debates would be pointless. For further discussion see: Erik Stenius, *Wittgenstein's Tractatus: A Critical Exposition of Its Main Lines of Thought* (Oxford: Basil Blackwell, 1960), pp. 179–180; H. R. G. Schwyzer, "Wittgenstein's Picture Theory of Language," in *Essays on Wittgenstein's Tractatus,* ed. Irving M. Copi and Robert W. Beard (New York: Macmillan, 1966), pp. 271–288; Stenius, "Wittgenstein's Picture Theory: A Reply to Mr. H. R. G. Schwyzer," in *Essays on Wittgenstein's "Tractatus,"* pp. 313–323; Max Black, *A Companion to Wittgenstein's "Tractatus"* (Ithaca, N.Y.: Cornell University Press, 1964), pp. 165–166; Donald Harward, *Wittgenstein's Saying and Showing Themes* (Bonn: Bouvier Verlag Herbert Grundmann, 1976), pp. 4–19; and Fogelin, *Wittgenstein,* pp. 86–88, 100–103.

5. Harward, *Saying and Showing,* pp. 6–8.

6. Ibid., p. 7.

7. The further distinction between what is without a sense *(sinnlos)* and what is nonsensical *(unsinnig),* though important, is not directly relevant to our concerns. In short, a pseudo-proposition about what is shown reflexively, e.g., logical form, Wittgenstein calls *sinnlos,* where *Unsinn* is what violates logical syntax and can neither be said nor shown. For a good discussion of this distinction see Max Black, *A Companion to Wittgenstein's "Tractatus,"* pp. 160–161.

8. Anthony Kenny, *Wittgenstein* (Cambridge, Mass.: Harvard University Press, 1973), pp. 43–44.

9. G. E. Moore, *British Academy Proceedings* 25 (1939): 273–300.

10. Moore, *Contemporary British Philosophy, 2d Series,* ed. J. H. Muirhead (New York: Macmillan, 1939), pp. 193–223.

11. For a fuller expression of this idea see OC #133.

12. Likewise, the expression "I know" sounds crazy when there is no indication of what could serve as proper grounds: "I am sitting with a philosopher in the garden; he says again and again 'I know that that's a tree', pointing to a tree that is near us. Someone else arrives and hears this, and I tell him: 'This fellow isn't insane. We are only doing philosophy'" (OC, #467).

13. The significance of this idea is supported by the fact it is repeated four times in the *Notebooks* (on page 2, remarks 2,3 and 5, and page 11 remark 4), is called in one instance "an extremely profound and important insight," and eventually finds its way into the *Tractatus* at 5.473.

14. Much of Oxford "ordinary language" analysis was built on this misunderstanding.

15. A blunt expression of the connection between doing metaphysics and failing to respect the say/show distinction appears in *Zettel:* "The essential thing about metaphysics: it obliterates the distinction between factual and conceptual investigations" (Wittgenstein, *Zettel,* ed. G. E. M. Anscombe and G. H. von Wright, trans. G. E. M. Anscombe [Berkeley and Los Angeles: University of California Press, 1967], remark #458; hereafter cited in text as Z).

16. Those wishing to defend the legitimacy of philosophy may dispute Wittgenstein's contention that philosophical discourses fail to constitute their own language-games. For a brief discussion of this issue see Robert J. Fogelin's *Wittgenstein,* 2d ed. (London: Routledge & Kegan Paul, 1987), pp. 141–142.

17. Pears, *Ludwig Wittgenstein,* pp. 95–104.

18. Ibid., p. 95.

19. Ibid., p. 96.

20. Ibid.

21. Ibid.

22. Ibid., p. 96.

23. Ibid., p. 102. Some later commentators adopt Pears' distinction and even seem to use his words to describe it. W. D. Hudson writes that "[Wittgenstein's] attention thus turned from the external limits to the internal subdivisions of language" (*Wittgenstein and Religious Belief* [New York: St. Martin's Press, 1975], p. 14), and Alan Keightley writes, "In the *Investigations* nonsense is produced by crossing an internal boundary without crossing it completely" (*Wittgenstein, Grammar and God* [London: Epworth Press, 1976], p. 56). Also see Alan P. F. Sell, review of W. D. Hudson's *Wittgenstein and Religious Belief, Philosophical Studies* 25 (1977): p. 380.

24. James Edwards, *Ethics Without Philosophy: Wittgenstein and the Moral Life* (Tampa: University Presses of Florida, 1982), pp. 142–143.

25. Ibid., p. 143.

26. Ibid., p. 142.

27. Garth Hallett, *A Companion to Wittgenstein's "Philosophical Investigations"* (Ithaca, N.Y.: Cornell University Press, 1977), p. 227.

28. Edwards, pp. 103–159.

29. Ibid., p. 109.

30. Ibid., pp. 18–19.

31. Ibid., pp. 49–50.

32. Stephen Toulmin, "Ludwig Wittgenstein" *Encounter* 32 (January 1969): 62.

33. Ibid.

34. Ibid., p. 63.

35. Immanuel Kant, *Critique of Pure Reason,* trans. Norman Kemp Smith (New York: St. Martin's Press, 1965), p. 24 (B xx).

36. Ibid., p. 29.

3. The Fearful Judge

1. Georg H. von Wright, "A Biographical Sketch," *Philosophical Review* vol. 64, no. 4 (1955): p. 543.

2. Ludwig Wittgenstein, *Lectures and Conversations on Aesthetics, Psychology and Religious Belief,* ed. Cyril Barrett, compiled from notes taken by Yorick Smythies, Rush Rhees and James Taylor (Berkeley: University of California Press, n.d.), p. 53; hereafter cited in text as LC.

3. The distinction Wittgenstein makes between "showing" and "saying" is discussed extensively in chapter 2, pp. 11–21.

4. Brian McGuinness, *Wittgenstein, a Life: Young Ludwig (1889–1921)* (Berkeley and Los Angeles: University of California Press, 1988), p. 47.

5. For an account of this episode see Hermine Wittgenstein, "My Brother Ludwig," *Recollections of Wittgenstein,* ed. Rush Rhees (Oxford: Oxford University Press, 1984), pp. 6–8.

6. See, for example, Norman Malcolm, *Ludwig Wittgenstein: A Memoir,* with a biographical sketch by G. H. von Wright and with Wittgenstein's letters to Malcolm, 2d ed. (Oxford: Oxford University Press, 1984).

7. This phrase was offered as a description of Wittgenstein's perfectionism by Stephen Toulmin, personal communication, September, 1988.

8. Kolakowski argues emphatically that Dostoevsky's maxim is valid both as a moral rule and an epistemological principle (Leszek Kolakowski, *Religion* [New York: Oxford University Press, 1982], p. 82).

9. James Gustafson, *Ethics from a Theological Perspective,* vol. 1 of *Theology and Ethics* (Chicago: University of Chicago Press, 1981), p. 167.

10. Taking the later concept of "forms of life" as the rightful heir of the earlier notion of "the world" is less obvious, perhaps, than taking "logical grammar" as the rightful heir of "logical form." Like "the world," the phrase "forms of life" refers to Wittgenstein's fundamental ontology: "What has to be accepted, the given, is—so one could say—*forms of life*" (PI, p. 226). Furthermore, both are defined, à la Schopenhauer, by the limits of language. In the *Tractatus* Wittgenstein claims that the limits of one's language mean the limits of one's world (TLP, 5.6; TLP, 5.62), and in the *Investigations* he remarks: "And to imagine a language means to imagine a form of life" (PI, #19).

11. David Pears, *Ludwig Wittgenstein* (Cambridge, Mass.: Harvard University Press, 1986), p. 147.

12. McGuinness, *A Life,* p. 293.

13. Paul Engelmann, *Letters from Ludwig Wittgenstein, With a Memoir,* ed. B. F. McGuinness, trans. L. Furtmüller (New York: Horizon Press, 1967), p. 33; quoted by

McGuinness, *A Life*, p. 293. Letter from Wittgenstein was dated by the recipient as 21 June 1920.

14. Malcolm, *A Memoir*, pp. 76–77.

15. Richard Polt brought this objection to my attention.

16. In the *Investigations* Wittgenstein no longer speaks of "agreement with the world" but of "agreement in forms of life" (PI, #241), though this could still be spoken of as "agreement with that alien will on which I appear dependent."

17. Gustafson, *Theology and Ethics*, p. 81.

18. Ibid., p. 9.

19. Ibid., p. 15.

20. Ibid., p. 99.

21. Ibid., p. 41.

22. Ibid., p. 16.

23. Ibid., p. 20.

24. Pears, *Ludwig Wittgenstein*, p. 179.

25. Pears seems close to recognizing this point when he argues that Wittgenstein's "anthropocentrism" should not be understood in opposition to "objectivism" (*Wittgenstein*, pp. 181–182).

26. Ludwig Wittgenstein, "Wittgenstein's Lecture on Ethics," *Philosophical Review* 74 (June 1967): 311–339; hereafter cited in text as LE.

27. Gustafson, *Theology and Ethics*, p. 81.

28. Ackermann's notion of a "one-step hermeneutic" is discussed in chapter 2, pp. 28–29.

29. In chapter 5, I will examine more extensively the role wonder plays in Wittgenstein's thought.

30. Wittgenstein invites this distinction by calling Ethics—together with pseudo-propositions about logical form—*sinnlos* (without sense), whereas "propositions" that violate logical grammar are simply called *unsinnig* (nonsensical). Most commentators have been understandably skeptical of making what amounts to a distinction between kinds of nonsense.

31. Gustafson, *Theology and Ethics*, p. 181.

32. I take what appears in the quotes to be Wittgenstein's voice, as though it were roughly equivalent to what normally appears in brackets, that is, as something that warrants further development.

33. Quoted by Leszek Kolakowski (Religion [New York: Oxford University Press, 1982], p. 43).

34. Gustafson, *Theology and Ethics*, p. 90.

35. Gen. 22:1–19.

36. Søren Kierkegaard, *Fear and Trembling*, and *The Sickness Unto Death*, trans. Walter Lowrie, 1st ed., rev. (Garden City, N.Y.: Doubleday, 1954), pp. 21–132.

37. "Notes on Talks with Wittgenstein," taken by Friedrich Waismann and published as a commentary immediately following Wittgenstein's "Lecture on Ethics," *Philosophical Review* 74 (June 1967): 15.

38. The German *Willkürlich*, which Anscombe has translated as "arbitrary" in the English edition of the *Investigations*, shares a similar ambiguity. Although it usually implies a degree of high-handedness, it is derived from *Willkür*, which in addition to

meaning "arbitrariness" or "caprice," can also mean "discretion" or "decree," which implies that the matter is settled and the direction set not irresponsibly but without reference to argument and justification.

39. For extended discussions of this idea see W. D. Hudson, *Wittgenstein and Religious Belief,* p. 58; R. H. Bell, *Theology as Grammar* (Ph.D. diss., Yale University, 1968); and, most importantly, Alan Keightley, *Wittgenstein, Grammar and God,* especially the chapter entitled "Grammar and the Sense of Religious Belief," pp. 41–60.

4. The Specter of Sin

1. P. M. S. Hacker, *Insight and Illusion* (London: Oxford University Press, 1972).

2. Hacker, *Insight and Illusion,* pp. 128–129. While the discussions in the following five paragraphs are my own, they are clearly inspired by the analyses given by Hacker, pp. 129–135.

3. Here Wittgenstein makes a play on the word "picture" *(bild),* which is the same word he uses in the *Tractatus* to describe how a proposition represents a possible state of affairs in the world. In other words, it is as if he were to say, "A picture of language as pictures held us captive."

4. Hacker notes that this seems to be an error Wittgenstein associated with Russell (*Insight and Illusion,* p. 133).

5. Published immediately following Wittgenstein's "Lecture on Ethics" in *Philosophical Review* 74 (June 1967): 12.

6. M. O'C. Drury, "Conversations with Wittgenstein," in *Recollections of Wittgenstein,* ed. Rush Rhees (Oxford: Oxford University Press, 1984), p. 105.

7. Gilbert Ryle quoted by Anthony Kenny in "Wittgenstein on the Nature of Philosophy" (*Wittgenstein and His Times,* ed. Brian McGuinness [Oxford: Basil Blackwell, 1982], p. 13).

8. Ibid., p. 12.

9. There seem to be three such references in *Philosophical Investigations:* #96, #110 and p. 215.

10. 1 Cor. 10:13.

11. *Summa Theologiae* 1–2.71.6.

12. André LaCocque, "Sin and Guilt," *The Encyclopedia of Religion,* ed. Mircea Eliade, 13:327.

13. Herodotus tells the story of Croesus, King of Lydia, who asked both the oracle at Delphi and the oracle at the shrine of Amphiaraus whether he would be victorious in his campaign against Cyrus of Persia. The oracles replied that if Croesus attacked the Persians he would destroy a mighty empire. Taking this as assurance of his victory, Croesus leads his armies into battle and is completely destroyed (*Histories* 1.53). Perhaps there was some arrogance in Croesus' assumption that the empire to be destroyed was Persian, and not his own, but as is typical in Greek tradition, the pronouncement of the oracle seems to be a test more of his cleverness than of his moral character.

14. Drury, "Conversations," in *Recollections,* ed. Rhees, p. 86.

15. Leo Tolstoy, *Twenty-Three Tales,* The World's Classics, vol. 72, trans. Louise Maude and Aylmer Maude (London: Oxford University Press, 1906), p. 201.

16. King, "Recollections of Wittgenstein," in *Recollections*, ed. Rhees, p. 72.

17. Quoted by Kenny in "Wittgenstein on the Nature of Philosophy," in *Wittgenstein*, ed. McGuinness, p. 14. I will continue the practice of referring to the unpublished manuscripts by the "MS" numbers given in G. H. von Wright's "The Wittgenstein Papers" (*Philosophical Review* 79 [1969]: 483–503).

18. The full meaning of this remark can best be understood in the context of Moore-type propositions. See, for example, OC #84: "Moore says he *knows* that the earth existed long before his birth. And put like that it seems to be a personal statement about him, even if it is in addition a statement about the physical world. Now it is philosophically uninteresting whether Moore knows this or that, but it is interesting that, and how, it can be known. If Moore had informed us that he knew the distance separating certain stars, we might conclude from that that he had made some special investigations, and we shall want to know what these were. But Moore chooses precisely a case in which we all seem to know the same as he, and without being able to say how."

19. Wittgenstein usually speaks of this kind of philosophy, philosophy gone wrong, by way of locutions like "when we do philosophy. . . ," or "when doing philosophy. . . ." See, for example, in the *Investigations* alone: #11, #131, #194, #261, #274, #295, #303, #348, #592, #598.

20. The full remark goes as follows: "Where does our investigation get its importance from, since it seems only to destroy everything interesting, that is, all that is great and important? (As it were all the buildings, leaving behind only bits of stone and rubble.) What we are destroying is nothing but houses of cards and we are clearing up the ground of language on which they stand" (PI, #18).

21. Quoted in Anthony Kenny, *Wittgenstein* (Cambridge: Harvard University Press, 1973), p. 13.

22. Ibid., p. 13.

23. Ibid., p. 15.

24. Leszek Kolakowski, *Religion* (New York: Oxford University Press, 1982), pp. 50–51.

25 Gasking and Jackson, "Wittgenstein as Teacher," *Ludwig Wittgenstein: The Man and His Philosophy*, ed. K. T. Fann (New Jersey: Harvester Press, 1967), p. 53, quoted by Fann in *Wittgenstein's Conception of Philosophy* (Berkeley and Los Angeles: University of California Press, 1971), p. 103–104.

26. Augustine Conf. 1.7.

27. These contrary impulses seem to correspond to the distinctive mix of extreme pride and self-disgust that biographers and memoirs frequently attribute to Wittgenstein, and in this too Wittgenstein is participating in a particular tradition. Karl Jaspers claims that an "arrogant humility" is a characteristic theme in Christian figures like St. Paul, St. Augustine, Pascal and Kierkegaard (*Plato and Augustine*, ed. Hannah Arendt, trans. Ralph Manheim [New York: Harcourt, Brace, 1962], p. 119).

28. Waismann, "Notes on Talks With Wittgenstein," *Philosophical Review* 74:16.

29. Rush Rhees makes a similar point in terms of what it means to accept or doubt the existence of God: "'God exists' is not a statement of fact. You might say also that it is not in the indicative mood. It is a confession—or expression—of faith. This is recognized in some way when people say that God's existence is 'necessary existence,'

as opposed to the 'contingency' of what exists as a matter of fact; and when they say that to doubt God's existence is a sin, as opposed to a mistake about the facts" (*Without Answers* [New York: Schocken Books, 1969], pp. 132–133).

The expression "God exists" in Rhees' analysis can be compared to the remark, "The world is there." Neither is a statement of fact, but they are both preconditions for facts. While it is open to question whether even the later Wittgenstein would condone the expression, "God exists," in the straightforward way Rhees describes, Wittgenstein would surely show it a measure of respect. Perhaps what he says about the remark, "The world is there," would apply toward the expression, "God exists," namely that what people mean when they say these kinds of things lies close to his heart.

30. McGuinness, "The Mysticism of the *Tractatus*," *Philosophical Review* 75 (1966): 317–318.

31. John Moran, *Toward the World and Wisdom of Wittgenstein's Tractatus*, Studies in Philosophy 26 (The Hague: Mouton & Co., 1973), p. 48. Moran also cites Paul Nizan's observation in *The Conspiracy*, trans. Quintin Hoare, with an afterword by Jean-Paul Sartre (London: Verso, 1988), p. 89, that nothing so hinders command as a soldier's suicide.

32. McGuinness suggests that Wittgenstein follows Schopenhauer in rejecting suicide as the supreme act of self-assertion of the will (Brian McGuinness, *Wittgenstein, A Life: Young Ludwig (1889–1921)* [Berkeley and Los Angeles: University of California Press, 1988], p. 254).

33. Gen. 11:4–8.

34. Rush Rhees argues that something is missing in the language first described in remark #2 of the *Philosophical Investigations*, namely, the further circumstances that determine how the activity of building fits into the rest of the builders' lives ("Wittgenstein's Builders," *Proceedings of the Aristotelian Society* 60 [1959–60]: 171–186). This wider picture helps to show whether the depth grammar is in order—it helps to show the difference between farming, for example, and building a tower to heaven.

35. Leo Tolstoy, *A Confession, The Gospel in Brief* and *What I Believe*, trans. with an intro. by Aylmer Maude (Oxford: Oxford University Press, 1940), p. 60.

36. Ibid., pp. 60–61.

37. For further discussion see chapter 2, pp. 20–21.

38. McGuinness, *A Life*, p. 130.

39. Wittgenstein, *Notebooks*, p. 76.

40. Weber suggests the German *Beruf* shares certain connotations with the English "calling," and he credits Luther and the Reformation for giving these connotations general currency (*The Protestant Ethic and the Spirit of Capitalism*, trans. Talcott Parsons, with an intro. by Anthony Giddens [London: Unwin Paperbacks, 1985], pp. 79–80).

41. Ibid., p. 80.

42. Weber speaks of Aquinas' notion that a vocation is taken up as a matter of *causae naturales,* citing *Quest. quodibetal* 7, Art. 17c. (Weber, *The Protestant Ethic,* p. 211).

43. Ibid., p. 81.

44. Wittgenstein's decision to be trained as an elementary school teacher after World War I, and to spend the next six years teaching in small rural schools in lower

Austria, could be seen in this light. Various memoirs by his friends and students speak of his later plan to go live and work in Russia (Pascal, "A Personal Memoir," in *Recollections,* ed. Rhees, pp. 26, 29–30; Drury, "Conversations," ibid., pp. 125–126; Rhees, "Postscript," ibid., pp. 198–200, 205–209), and his well known efforts to encourage his pupils to leave academia and take up manual skills or professions like engineering and medicine. See, for example, Norman Malcolm, *A Memoir and a Biographical Sketch by G. H. von Wright,* 2d ed. (Oxford: Oxford University Press, 1984), p. 28; Pascal, "A Personal Memoir," in *Recollections,* ed. Rhees, pp. 23–26; Drury, "Conversations," ibid., pp. 121–124. These efforts are all part of Wittgenstein's commitment to something resembling worldly asceticism. The importance he attached to adopting a vocation was primarily for the health of one's soul, and the idea of making a useful contribution to society was more of a by-product, in the Weberian sense, of spiritual concerns.

45. Tolstoy, *A Confession,* p. 61.

46. Ibid., p. 65.

47. Albert Camus, "Le Mythe de Sisyphe," in *Le Mythe de Sisyphe* (Paris: Gallimard, 1942), pp. 161–166.

48. This issue will be considered further in chapter 5, pp. 103–106.

49. Richard Lyman, *The Seven Deadly Sins: Society and Evil,* 1st rev. and expanded ed. (New York: General Hall, Inc., 1989), pp. 5–52.

50. Ibid., p. 5.

51. Morton Bloomfield, *The Seven Deadly Sins: An Introduction to the History of a Religious Concept* (East Lansing, Michigan: Michigan State University Press, 1967), pp. 57–60; cited in Lyman, *The Seven Deadly Sins,* p. 6.

52. Bloomfield, pp. 229–232; cited in Lyman, *The Seven Deadly Sins,* p. 7.

53. Lyman, *The Seven Deadly Sins,* p. 7.

54. Ibid.

55. Tolstoy, *A Confession,* pp. 58, 60.

56. Lyman, *The Seven Deadly Sins,* p. 30.

57. Ibid., p. 6.

58. See the entire work entitled *The Sickness Unto Death,* bound in the double volume *Fear and Trembling* and *The Sickness Unto Death,* trans. Walter Lowrie, 1st ed., rev. (Garden City, N.Y.: Doubleday, 1954).

59. Perhaps this is why some nonsense stories, especially those penned under the name of Lewis Carroll, lend themselves to the teaching of elementary logic. For a discussion of some similarities between Wittgenstein and Lewis Carroll in their treatment of nonsense, see George Pitcher, "Wittgenstein, Nonsense and Lewis Carroll," in *Ludwig Wittgenstein: The Man and His Philosophy,* ed. K. T. Fann (New Jersey: Humanities Press, 1967), pp. 315–335.

60. Quoted by Kenny, "Wittgenstein on the Nature of Philosophy," in *Wittgenstein,* ed. McGuinness, p. 5.

61. Exod. 20: 1–5.

62. Augustine Conf. 2.6.

63. Gustafson, *Theology and Ethics,* p. 296.

64. "Wittgenstein and the Theory of Types," in *Perspectives on the Philosophy of Wittgenstein,* ed. Irving Block (Cambridge, Mass.: MIT Press, 1981), p. 45.

65. Although the treatment of relations is stated here rather cryptically, it is intimately tied to other more developed themes like the picture-theory, and it is already implied in the opening lines of the *Tractatus*. For example, when Wittgenstein declares, "The world is the totality of facts, not of things" (TLP, 1.1), he means to point out from the start that objects never exist as an unstructured list of things, but objects always exist in some determinate relation to other objects. In other words, there is no need to posit a third thing, a relation, which would transform two isolated objects into a determinate structure.

66. Robert Fogelin, *Wittgenstein*, 2d ed. (London: Routledge & Kegan Paul, 1987), p. 41.

67. Michael Dummett argues that Wittgenstein's direct criticisms of Frege's doctrine of assertion generally miss the mark ("Frege and Wittgenstein," in *Perspectives*, ed. Block, p. 33).

68. Compare this to PI, #22.

69. These remarks are, of course, intertwined with the whole set of difficult issues surrounding the notion of private language. But there is no need to address these issues here, since their outcome would have no bearing on the strength or weakness of describing Wittgenstein's treatment of mental phenomena in terms of an effort to destroy idols.

70. Gustafson, *Theology and Ethics*, p. 296.

5. Writing to the Glory of God

1. M. O'C. Drury, "Some Notes on Conversations," in *Recollections of Wittgenstein*, ed. Rush Rhees (Oxford University Press, 1984), pp. 79, 160.

2. Georg H. von Wright, "Wittgenstein in Relation to His Times," in *Wittgenstein and His Times*, ed. McGuinness, (Oxford: Basil Blackwell, 1982), p. 119.

3. See, for example, the preface to the *Philosophical Investigations*, p. vi.

4. J. C. Nyíri, "Wittgenstein's Later Work in Relation to Conservatism," *Wittgenstein*, ed. McGuinness, pp. 44–68.

5. McGuinness, "Freud and Wittgenstein," ibid., p. 41.

6. Von Wright, "Wittgenstein in Relation to His Times," ibid., p. 116.

7. McGuinness, "Freud and Wittgenstein," ibid., p. 41.

8. Drury, "Conversations," *Recollections*, ed. Rhees, p. 79.

9. Von Wright, "Wittgenstein in Relation to His Times," in *Wittgenstein*, ed. McGuinness, p. 115.

10. Quoted by von Wright, ibid.

11. In a letter to Drury Wittgenstein expresses this attitude in human terms: "You said in the Park yesterday that possibly you had made a mistake in having taken up medicine: you immediately added that probably it was wrong to think such a thing at all. I am sure it is. But not because being a doctor you may not go the wrong way, or go to the dogs, but because if you do, this has nothing to do with your choice of a profession being a mistake. For what human being can say what would have been the right thing if this is the wrong one? You didn't make a mistake because there was nothing at the time you knew or ought to have known that you overlooked. Only this one could have called making a mistake; and even if you had made a mistake in this sense, this would now have to be regarded as a datum as all the other circumstances

inside and outside which you can't alter (control). The thing now is to live in the world in which you are, not to think or dream about the world you would like to be in" (Drury, "Some Notes on Conversations," *Recollections*, ed. Rhees, pp. 95–96).

12. James Edwards suggests that *Äußerung* is best rendered "a trusting grasp" (*Ethics Without Philosophy: Wittgenstein and the Moral Life* [Tampa, Fla.: University Presses Florida, 1982], pp. 183, 196).

13. It is just this confusion which gives rise to idle metaphysical speculations: "The essential thing about metaphysics: it obliterates the distinction between factual and conceptual investigations" (Z, #458).

14. See for example, Kai Nielsen, "Wittgensteinian Fideism," *Philosophy*, vol. 42, no. 161 (July 1967): 191–209.

15. After Wittgenstein declares that we must replace our explanations with descriptions, he continues: "And this description gets its light, that is to say its purpose, from the philosophical problems" (PI, #109).

16. The imagined tribe which consults an oracle when we would consult a physicist is a more difficult case. It certainly seems to us that our preference here is well founded and not just a reflection of our customs, but for Wittgenstein the point is the same. Considered theoretically there is no way to choose between our way and the way of the imagined tribe, but in fact one way *is* compelling for us and the other is not. This is a straightforward remark about the grammar of our language, about what it requires of us. Any further assertions and speculations about the *ultimate* value of one grammar versus another are vain and futile. Wittgenstein denies us any grounds for going on to say, "but any disinterested observer would surely agree that our way is better, that it reflects the truth of how things are." He would consider the notion of a disinterested observer a misguided Cartesian myth, and anything less would just be a matter of "using our language-game as a base from which to combat theirs," in which case we have returned to the basic fact that we find our way compelling (OC, #609).

17. Drury, "Conversations," in *Recollections*, ed. Rhees, p. 79.

18. John 10:26.

19. Leszak Kolakowski, *Religion* (New York: Oxford University Press, 1982), p. 182.

20. Ibid., p. 54.

21. The particular Calvinist mechanism Weber describes, whereby worldly asceticism is intensified by the individual's desire to prove his election via success in his vocation, does not seem to have a direct application in Wittgenstein's case. While Weber sees this as the most intense form of worldly asceticism, it should not obscure his argument that worldly asceticism is a much larger phenomenon that characterizes the Judeo-Christian tradition as a whole.

22. Quoted in Rhees, "Wittgenstein on Language and Ritual," in *Wittgenstein*, ed. McGuinness, p. 92.

23. Weber emphasizes that in its extreme form, worldly asceticism means one does not just remain in the world literally, sequestered in monasteries or protected by ecclesiastical institutions, but one must remain in worldly occupations and institutions. This tends to encourage a priestless religion where each person has to work out his or her own salvation, and where the only way to do the will of God is to work in one's

"calling." Consequently, each calling has the same religious value and, if anything, work in a worldly occupation is preferable to work in a church. Drury reports a conversation when Wittgenstein said: "For all you and I can tell, the religion of the future will be without any priests or ministers. I think one of the things you and I have to learn is that we have to live without the consolation of belonging to a Church. If you feel you must belong to some organization, why don't you join the Quakers?"

The next day Wittgenstein retracted this recommendation—"As if nowadays any one organization was better than another,"—and went on to assert: "Of one thing I am certain. The religion of the future will have to be extremely ascetic; and by that I don't mean just going without food and drink." Troubled by this remark, Drury writes: "I seemed to sense for the first time in my life the idea of an asceticism of the intellect; that this life of reading and discussing in the comfort of Cambridge society, which I so enjoyed, was something I would have to renounce" (Drury, "Conversations," *Recollections*, ed. Rhees, p. 114).

24. Rush Rhees recalls an exchange Wittgenstein had in 1943 with Professor Farrington, who had just delivered a paper on "Causal Laws and History" at a meeting of the College Philosophical Society in Swansea:

> In the discussion Wittgenstein said that when there is a change in the conditions in which people live, we may call it progress because it opens up new possibilities. But in the course of this change, opportunities which were there before may be lost. In one way it was progress, in another it was decline. A historical change may be progress and also be ruin. There is no method of weighing one against the other to justify you in speaking of "progress on the whole."
>
> Farrington did not see how progress could also be ruin. What would be an example of this?
>
> Wittgenstein: "Why, just what you described when you said that the mining of iron and coal made it possible for industry to develop and at the same time scarred the valley with slag-heaps and old machinery."
>
> Farrington thought this was not a reason against saying that there has been progress on the whole. "With all the ugly sides of our civilization, I am sure I would rather live as we do now than have to live as the caveman did."
>
> Wittgenstein: "Yes of course you would. But would the caveman?"
> (Rhees, "Postscript," in *Recollections*, ed. Rhees, p. 201).

25. From an unpublished typescript from the early thirties known as the "Big Typescript." Quoted without specific citation by Anthony Kenny in "Wittgenstein on the Nature of Philosophy," in *Wittgenstein,* ed. McGuinness, p. 7.

26. The object of this rebuke was also a monk, so McGuinness uses it to illustrate Wittgenstein's attitude toward institutional religion during his student days at Cambridge (Pinsent's Diary, Nov. 9, 1912, quoted in McGuinness, *Wittgenstein, A Life: Young Ludwig (1889–1921)* [Berkeley and Los Angeles: University of California Press, 1988], p. 111).

27. Drury, "Conversations," in *Recollections,* ed. Rhees, p. 147.

28. Citing a letter Wittgenstein wrote to Moritz Schlick (LW to MS, 8 August 1932), McGuinness stresses that "the *Tractatus* is directed as much against the meta-

physics of the physicists (physicalism) as against that of the philosophers (of which phenomenalism would be one form)" (McGuinness, *A Life*, p. 314).

29. Hence Wittgenstein shows great distrust and disgust with books and public lectures which oversimplify various scientific ideas or discoveries in an effort to popularize science. When Drury once mentioned Sir James Jeans' *The Mysterious Universe*, Wittgenstein declared: "These books which attempt to popularize science are an abomination. They pander to people's curiosity to be titillated by the wonders of science without having to do any of the really hard work involved in understanding what science is about. Now a good book is one like Faraday's *The Chemical History of a Candle*. Faraday takes a simple phenomenon like a candle burning, and shows how complicated a process it really is" (Drury, "Conversations," *Recollections*, ed. Rhees, p. 117).

In his "Lectures on Aesthetics" Wittgenstein even objects to the title of Jeans' book: "I might say the title *The Mysterious Universe* includes a kind of idol worship, the idol being Science and the Scientist" (LC, p. 27).

30. Quoted in Rhees, "Wittgenstein on Language and Ritual," in *Wittgenstein*, ed. McGuinness, p. 93.

31. Wittgenstein, *Remarks on Frazer's "Golden Bough,"* ed. Rush Rhees, trans. A. C. Miles and rev. Rush Rhees (Doncaster, England: Brynmill Press Ltd., 1979), p. 17; hereafter cited in text as RFGB.

32. D. Z. Phillips uses this passage to begin a paper entitled "Wittgenstein's Full Stop," where he suggests that Wittgenstein's discussion of the difficulty of stopping, the urge to go beyond a certain point in a search for explanations, justifications and foundations, should be related to his religious views (*Perspectives on the Philosophy of Wittgenstein*, ed. Irving Block [Cambridge, Mass.: MIT Press, 1981], pp. 179–200).

33. McGuinness, *A Life*, p. 56.

34. Most of those to whom Wittgenstein confessed have died without ever revealing the content of these confessions. The most complete account in print is in Fania Pascal, "A Personal Memoir," *Recollections*, ed. Rhees, pp. 34–39. There is also a brief comment in Drury, "Conversations," ibid., p. 120.

35. This kind of juxtaposition has often encouraged the premature notion of "two Wittgensteins," and it is worth discussing in more detail.

In the two passages mentioned above, Wittgenstein unfortunately draws on the same "ladder" metaphor to express the two opposing aspects of his fundamental position, a position analogous to what Weber calls worldly asceticism. Although Wittgenstein's ideas underwent many transformations in this period, there is a deep continuity in terms of his fundamental view of the world, and both of the opposing aspects of worldly asceticism are as clearly present in the *Tractatus* as they are in the writings from the early 1930s. It is true that in the *Tractatus* the need for a ladder indicates a disenchantment with the world, a sense that something is wrong with us as we naturally stand. However, the fact that we are ultimately meant to throw the ladder away is another way of saying that the place to which it takes us is where we were all along, and in this sense the ladder does not presume to help us escape the world or to change how things are. Our problem is rooted in a perverse will which blinds us to what is right before our eyes, and the ladder is merely a means to tear away the veil of self-deception so we can see the world aright. In this same sense the whole of the *Philosophical Investigations* is meant to be a ladder that is thrown away after it is climbed. Wittgenstein's later philosophy still "leaves everything as it is" (PI, #124), and it is only of use as a kind of therapy for those who have already become confused by philosophical ways of thinking.

All this refers to a completely different kind of ladder then the one being dismissed in 1930. In the later quote, the rejection of the ladder represents Wittgenstein's rejection of all props, scaffolds and other artificial contrivances which try to raise us above the world to a place for which we are ill-suited, to where the atmosphere is too thin to breathe—much as the Protestant movement rejected the monastic life and its efforts to live somewhere between heaven and earth in a provisional escape from the world. In terms of Wittgenstein's later writings, this kind of ladder represents our recourse to theories and explanations that solve nothing and even exacerbate our problems by separating us from the routine activities and language-games that constitute our forms of life, effectively removing our feet from the ground which supports and sustains us.

This, of course, is a constant theme throughout Wittgenstein's writings. He might easily have used the 1930s remark earlier in the *Tractatus* to express his rejection of Russell's intention to create an ideal language. The apparent contradiction between Wittgenstein's claim that his work is a ladder that must be thrown away after it is climbed, and his claim that anything that can be reached by a ladder does not interest him, hinges on an equivocation in the term "ladder" and not on a fundamental change in his view of the world.

36. Rhees, "Postscript," in *Recollections,* ed. Rhees, p. 190.

37. Pears, *Wittgenstein,* p. 187.

38. In the *Investigations,* Wittgenstein refers with approval to a conversation where F. P. Ramsey emphasized that logic was a "normative science" (PI, #81).

39. D. Z. Phillips, *Faith and Philosophical Enquiry* (London: Routledge and Kegan Paul, 1970), p. 165.

40. Gustafson, *Theology and Ethics,* p. 167.

41. Actually this comparison implies an oversimplification of pragmatism, as well as of Wittgenstein. American pragmatism—as represented by figures like Peirce, James, Royce and Dewey—does not simply reduce everything to questions of utility. I would further suggest that there is a moral dimension underlying the entire pragmatist tradition, and that its deep attraction to science frequently has religious motivations.

42. Frazer's original remark, supplied in a footnote by Rush Rhees: "The same principle of make-believe, so dear to children, has led other peoples to employ a simulation of birth as a form of adoption. . . . A woman will take a boy whom she intends to adopt and push or pull him through her clothes; ever afterwards he is regarded as her very son, and inherits the whole property of his adoptive parents" (James George Frazer, *The Golden Bough,* vol. 1: *The Magic Art* [New York: Macmillan, 1935], p. 74).

43. There is a clear danger in speaking of language-games as rituals. Although Wittgenstein seems to find it easy to respect the rituals of "primitive" societies, he is very suspicious of the rituals found in contemporary religious practices, and in his own life he could never bring himself to participate in institutional religion. He had a sense that there is something false or disingenuous about rituals in the context of modern religious institutions, and on one occasion he wrote: "Everything ritual (everything high-priestly, as it were) must be strictly avoided, because it immediately turns bad. A kiss, to be sure, is also a ritual, and does not go bad—but the only allowable ritual is what is as genuine

as a kiss" (MS, 109, 208–209, quoted by Rhees, "Wittgenstein on Language and Ritual," in *Wittgenstein,* ed. McGuinness, p. 92). When I suggest that language-games in general can be compared to rituals, it must be the spontaneous rituals of everyday—rituals which are "as genuine as a kiss"—that are the object of comparison, and not the "high-priestly" rituals found in many of our modern religious practices.

44. Edwards, *Ethics Without Philosophy,* p. 163.

45. Augustine Conf. 1.1.

46. Rev. 3:15–16.

47. Gustafson, *Theology and Ethics,* p. 167.

48. Weber claims this led to the rationalization of the world *(Rationalisierung der Welt),* where every aspect of life for the faithful was regulated by disciplined routines, which in turn created a reliable and long-suffering work force for the industrial revolution. Weber was clearly aware of the irony in the fact that an intensification and generalization of religious life gave rise to an unprecedented pursuit and growth of materialism.

49. Fogelin, *Wittgenstein,* p. 209.

50. Drury, "Conversations," in *Recollections,* ed. Rhees, p. 79.

51. This is discussed at length in chapter 4, pp. 70-71.

52. James Edwards argues that the way that the world in the *Tractatus* can only conform to our will by a "grace of fate," is an antecedent of seeing the world as a miracle *(Ethics Without Philosophy,* pp. 38–41).

53. In the "Lecture on Ethics" Wittgenstein is acutely aware of this tension, and he sums it up in Kierkegaardian terms: "It is the paradox that an experience, a fact, should seem to have supernatural value" (LE, p. 10).

54. Occasionalism, as I understand it here, centers around the idea that there is no power or force in things themselves and that it is only the efficacy of the will of God that preserves the existence of things and produces the appearance of the self-same body from moment to moment whether at rest or in motion.

While I find the comparison to occasionalism important and illuminating, it is with a clear sense of the risk involved in making such comparisons. Wittgenstein was generally careful not to take over the ideas and doctrines of his predecessors wholesale, when he took them at all, and he was fastidious about avoiding the obvious pitfalls of the well-known schools of thought. As Baker reminds us, Wittgenstein "seldom ever mentions an 'ism' at all. When his imaginary or real interlocutors used any such label for his ideas, he invariably treated this as a symptom of misunderstanding. When he spoke of 'isms', he always took them as targets of criticism (finitism in the *Lectures on the Foundations of Mathematics,* nominalism in *Philisophical Grammar* and behaviourism in *Investigations*)" (Gorden Baker, *Wittgenstein, Frege and the Vienna Circle* [Oxford: Basil Blackwell, 1988], p. 256). I take this risk because the notion of genius creating original thoughts out of nothing is an ideology that is even more dangerous and inclined to abuse. The thrust of this book is that there are many important continuities between Wittgenstein and earlier thinkers and traditions and that to ignore or dismiss these continuities because of their generality or imperfection is only to introduce unnecessary obscurity and mystification.

55. Rush Rhees, *Without Answers,* Studies in Ethics and the Philosophy of Religion (New York: Schocken Books, 1969), p. 119.

56. Wittgenstein and Heidegger appear to agree as to the centrality and importance of this question, though they approach it in different ways. In the "Lecture on
Ethics" Wittgenstein suggests that our wonder at the existence of the world is the kind
of experience which gives rise to our notion of absolute value, and he goes on to say:
"I am then inclined to use such phrases as 'how extraordinary that anything should
exist' or 'how extraordinary that the world should exist'" (LE, p. 8). At the end of his
lecture "What Is Metaphysics," Heidegger poses the most fundamental question in
metaphysics as follows: "Why is there any Being at all—why not far rather Nothing?"
("What is Metaphysics?" *Basic Writings,* ed. David Farrell Krell [San Francisco: Harper
& Row, 1977], p. 112).

SELECTED BIBLIOGRAPHY

Ackermann, Robert John. 1988. *Wittgenstein's City.* Amherst, Mass.: University of Massachusetts Press.

Anscombe, G. E. M. 1959. *An Introduction to Wittgenstein's Tractatus.* London: Hutchinson University Library.

Augustine, Saint. 1984. *City of God.* Translated by Henry Bettenson. With an Introduction by John O'Meara. New York: Viking Penguin.

_____. 1963. *The Confessions of St. Augustine.* Translated by Rex Warner. New York: New American Library.

Baker, Gorden. 1984. *Wittgenstein, Frege and the Vienna Circle.* Oxford: Basil Blackwell.

Baker, G. P. and Hacker, P. M. S. 1984. *Skepticism, Rules and Language.* Oxford: Basil Blackwell.

_____. 1980. *Wittgenstein: Understanding and Meaning.* Vol. 1, *An Analytical Commentary on the "Philosophical Investigations."* Chicago: University of Chicago Press.

_____. 1985. *Wittgenstein: Rules, Grammar and Necessity.* Vol. 2, *An Analytical Commentary on the "Philosophical Investigations."* Oxford: Basil Blackwell.

Barrett, Cyril. 1991. *Wittgenstein, Ethics and Religious Belief.* Oxford: Basil Blackwell.

Bartley, W. W., III. 1981. *Wittgenstein.* 2d ed. LaSalle, Ill.: Open Court.

Black, Max. 1964. *A Companion to Wittgenstein's "Tractatus."* Ithaca, N.Y.: Cornell University Press.

Block, Irving, ed. 1981. *Perspectives on the Philosophy of Wittgenstein.* Cambridge, Mass.: MIT Press.

Bouwsma, O. K. 1986. *Wittgenstein: Conversations 1949–1951.* Edited with an Introduction by Craft, J. L., and Hustwit, Ronald E. Indianapolis, Ind.: Hackett Publishing Company.

Brand, Gerd. 1979. *The Essential Wittgenstein.* Translated with an Introduction by Robert E. Innis. New York: Basic Books, Inc.

Cavell, Stanley. 1979. *The Claim of Reason: Wittgenstein, Skepticism, Morality and Tragedy.* Oxford: Oxford University Press.

_____. 1976. *Must We Mean What We Say?* Cambridge: Cambridge University Press.

Copi, Irving M., and Beard, Robert W., eds. 1966. *Essays on Wittgenstein's "Tractatus."* New York: Macmillan.

D'hert O. P., Ignace. 1974. *Wittgenstein's Relevance for Theology.* European University Papers, Series 23: Theology, Vol. 44. Bern: Herbert Lang & Co. Ltd.

Drury, M. O'C. 1973. *The Danger of Words*. New York: Humanities Press.

Edwards, James. 1982. *Ethics Without Philosophy: Wittgenstein and the Moral Life*. Tampa, Fla.: University Presses of Florida.

Engelmann, Paul. 1967. *Letters from Ludwig Wittgenstein, With a Memoir*. Edited by B. F. McGuinness. Translated by L. Furtmüller. New York: Horizon Press.

Fann, K. T., ed. 1967. *Ludwig Wittgenstein: The Man and His Philosophy*. New Jersey: Harvester Press.

_____. 1971. *Wittgenstein's Conception of Philosophy*. Berkeley and Los Angeles: University of California Press.

Ferré, Fredrick. 1961. *Language, Logic and God*. New York: Harper. Reprint. Chicago: University of Chicago Press, 1981.

Findlay, J. N. 1984. *Wittgenstein: A Critique*. London: Routledge & Kegan Paul.

Fogelin, Robert J. 1987. *Wittgenstein*. 2d ed. London: Routledge & Kegan Paul.

Frazer, Sir James G. 1935. *The Golden Bough*. New York: Macmillan.

Frege, Gottlob. 1952. *Philosophical Writings of Gottlob Frege*. Translated by Peter Geach and Max Black. Oxford: Basil Blackwell.

Grayling, A. C. 1988. *Wittgenstein*. Oxford: Oxford University Press.

Gustafson, James. 1981. *Ethics from a Theocentric Perspective*. Vol. 1, *Theology and Ethics*. Chicago: University of Chicago Press.

Hacker, P. M. S. 1972. *Insight and Illusion*. London: Oxford University Press.

_____. 1990. *Wittgenstein: Meaning and Mind*. Vol. 3, *An Analytical Commentary on the "Philosophical Investigations."* Oxford: Basil Blackwell.

Hallet, Garth. 1977. *A Companion to Wittgenstein's "Philosophical Investigations."* Ithaca, N.Y.: Cornell University Press.

Heidegger, Martin. 1977. "What Is Metaphysics?" *Basic Writings*. Translated by David Farrell Krell. San Francisco: Harper & Row.

High, Dallas M. 1967. *Language, Persons, and Belief*. New York: Oxford University Press.

_____, ed. 1969. *New Essays on Religious Language*. New York: Oxford University Press.

Hintikka, Merrill B., and Hintikka, Jaakko. 1986. *Investigating Wittgenstein*. Oxford: Basil Blackwell.

Hordern, William. 1964. *Speaking of God*. New York: Macmillan.

Hudson, W. Donald. 1975. *Wittgenstein and Religious Belief*. New Studies in the Philosophy of Religion. New York: St. Martin's Press.

Hutchison, John A. 1963. *Language and Faith*. Philadelphia: Westminster Press.

International Wittgenstein Symposium, 2d, Kirchberg, Austria, 1977. 1978. "Wittgenstein and His Impact on Contemporary Thought." Edited by Elisabeth Leinfellner, Werner Leinfellner, Hal Berghel, and Adolf Hübner. Vienna: Hölder-Pichler-Tempsky.

James, William. N.d. *The Varieties of Religious Experience: A Study in Human Nature*. Being the Gifford Lectures on Natural Religion Delivered at Edinburgh in 1901–1902. With a Foreword by Jacques Barzun. New York: New American Library.

Janik, Allan, and Toulmin, Stephen. 1973. *Wittgenstein's Vienna*. New York: Simon and Schuster.

Jaspers, Karl. 1962. *Plato and Augustine.* Edited by Hannah Arendt. Translated by Ralph Manheim. New York: Harcourt, Brace & World.

Kant, Immanuel. 1929. *The Critique of Pure Reason.* Translated by Norman Kemp Smith. London: Macmillan.

_____. 1960. *Religion Within the Limits of Reason Alone.* Translated by Theodore M. Greene and Hoyt H. Hudson. With an essay by John Silber. New York: Harper.

Kenny, Anthony. 1987. *The Legacy of Wittgenstein.* Oxford: Basil Blackwell.

_____. 1973. *Wittgenstein.* Cambridge, Mass.: Harvard University Press.

Keightley, Alan. 1976. *Wittgenstein, Grammar and God.* London: Epworth Press.

Kierkegaard, Søren. 1954. *Fear and Trembling,* and *The Sickness Unto Death.* Translated by Walter Lowrie. 1st ed., rev. Garden City, N.Y.: Doubleday & Company.

Kolakowski, Leszek. 1982. *Religion.* New York: Oxford University Press.

Lazerowitz, Morris. 1977. *The Language of Philosophy: Freud and Wittgenstein.* Boston Studies in the Philosophy of Science, Vol. 55. Edited by Robert S. Cohen and Marx W. Wartofsky. Dordrecht, Holland: D. Reidel Publishing Company.

Luckhardt, C. G., ed. 1979. *Wittgenstein: Sources and Perspectives.* Ithaca, N.Y.: Cornell University Press.

Lyman, Stanford M. 1989. *The Seven Deadly Sins: Society and Evil.* 1st rev. and expanded ed. New York: General Hall, Inc.

Malcolm, Norman. 1984. *Ludwig Wittgenstein: A Memoir.* 2d ed. With a Biographical Sketch by G. H. von Wright. With Wittgenstein's Letters to Malcolm. Oxford: Oxford University Press.

_____. 1986. *Nothing is Hidden: Wittgenstein's Criticism of His Early Thought.* Oxford: Basil Blackwell.

McGuinness, Brian, ed. 1982. *Wittgenstein and His Times.* Oxford: Basil Blackwell.

_____. 1988. *Wittgenstein, A Life: Young Ludwig (1889–1921).* Berkeley, Los Angeles and London: University of California Press.

Monk, Ray. 1990. *Ludwig Wittgenstein: The Duty of Genius.* New York: The Free Press.

Moore, G. E. 1962. *Philosophical Papers.* New York: Collier Books.

Moran, John. 1973. *Toward the World and Wisdom of Wittgenstein's "Tractatus."* Studies in Philosophy, Vol. 26. The Hague: Mouton & Co.

Morawetz, Thomas. 1978. *Wittgenstein and Knowledge.* Atlantic Highlands, N.J.: Humanities Press.

Mounce, H. O. 1981. *Wittgenstein's Tractatus.* Chicago: University of Chicago Press.

Pears, David. 1987. *The False Prison.* 2 vols. Oxford: Clarendon Press.

_____. 1986. *Ludwig Wittgenstein.* Cambridge, Mass.: Harvard University Press.

Phillips, D. Z. 1970. *Faith and Philosophical Enquiry.* London: Routledge & Kegan Paul.

Pitcher, George, ed. 1966. *Wittgenstein: The Philosophical Investigations.* Modern Studies in Philosophy. Notre Dame, Ind.: University of Notre Dame Press.

Pletsch, Carl. 1991. *Young Nietzsche: Becoming a Genius.* New York: The Free Press.

Pole, David. 1958. *The Later Philosophy of Wittgenstein.* London: Athlone Press.

Ramsey, Ian T. 1963. *On Being Sure in Religion.* London: Athlone Press.

Ricoeur, Paul. 1967. *The Symbolism of Evil.* Translated by Emerson Buchanan. New York: Harper and Row.

Rieff, Philip. 1987. *The Triumph of the Therapeutic.* Chicago: University of Chicago Press.

Rhees, Rush, ed. 1984. *Recollections of Wittgenstein.* Oxford: Oxford University Press.

Rhees, Rush. 1969. *Without Answers.* Studies in Ethics and the Philosophy of Religion. New York: Schocken Books.

Schopenhauer, Arthur. 1908. *Die beiden Grundprobleme der Ethik.* 5th ed. Leipzig: F. A. Brockhaus.

Sherry, Patrick. 1977. *Religion, Truth and Language-Games.* New York: Barnes & Noble.

Tilghman, Benjamin R. 1991. *Wittgenstein, Ethics and Aesthetics: The View from Eternity.* Albany: State University of New York Press.

Tolstoy, Leo. 1940. *A Confession, The Gospel in Brief* and *What I Believe.* Translated with an Introduction by Aylmer Maude. Oxford: Oxford University Press.

_____. 1906. *Twenty-Three Tales.* The World's Classics, Vol. 72. Translated by Louise Maude and Aylmer Maude. London: Oxford University Press.

Toulmin, Stephen. 1969. "Ludwig Wittgenstein." *Encounter* 32 (January): 58–71.

Waismann, Friedrich. 1979. *Wittgenstein and the Vienna Circle.* Oxford: Basil Blackwell.

Weber, Max. 1985. *The Protestant Ethic and the Spirit of Capitalism.* Translated by Talcott Parsons with an Introduction by Antony Giddens. London: Unwin Paperbacks.

Weininger, Otto. 1906. *Sex and Character.* Translator anonymous. London: Willian Heinemann.

Winch, Peter. 1972. *Ethics and Action.* London: Routledge and Kegan Paul.

Wittgenstein, Ludwig. 1980. *Culture and Value.* Edited by G. H. von Wright in collaboration with Heikki Nyman. Translated by Peter Winch. Chicago: University of Chicago Press.

_____. 1967. *Lectures and Conversations on Aesthetics, Psychology and Religious Belief.* Compiled from Notes taken by Yorick Smythies, Rush Rhees and James Taylor. Edited by Cyril Barrett. Berkeley and Los Angeles: University of California Press.

_____. 1974. *Letters to Russell, Keynes and Moore.* Edited with an Introduction by G. H. von Wright. Assisted by B. F. McGuinness. Ithaca, N.Y.: Cornell University Press.

_____. 1979. *Notebooks: 1914–1916.* 2d ed. Edited by G. H. von Wright and G. E. M. Anscombe. Translated by G. E. M. Anscombe. 2nd ed. Chicago: University of Chicago Press.

_____. 1969. *On Certainty.* Edited by G. E. M. Anscombe and G. H. von Wright. Translated by Denis Paul and G. E. M. Anscombe. New York: Harper and Row, Harper Torchbooks.

_____. 1953. *Philosophical Investigations.* Edited by G. H. von Wright and G. E. M. Anscombe. Translated by G. E. M. Anscombe. Oxford: Basil Blackwell.

_____. 1975. *Philosophical Remarks.* Edited by Rush Rhees. Translated by Raymond Hargreaves and Roger White. Chicago: University of Chicago Press.

_____. 1956. *Remarks on the Foundations of Mathematics.* Edited by G. H. von Wright, R. Rhees, G. E. M. Anscombe. Translated by G. E. M. Anscombe. Cambridge, Mass.: MIT Press.

_____. 1979. *Remarks on Frazer's "Golden Bough."* Edited by Rush Rhees. Translated by A. C. Miles and revised by Rush Rhees. Doncaster, England: Brynmill Press.

_____. 1961. *Tractatus Logico-Philosophicus.* Translated by D. F. Pears and B. F. McGuinness. With an Introduction by Bertrand Russell. London: Routledge and Kegan Paul.

_____. 1967. "Wittgenstein's Lecture on Ethics." *Philosophical Review* 74 (June): 311–339.

_____. 1967. *Zettel.* Edited by G. E. M. Anscombe and G. H. von Wright. Translated by G. E. M. Anscombe. Berkeley and Los Angeles: University of California Press.

INDEX